CHRISTIAN BAPTISM

by

JOHN MURRAY

Professor of Systematic Theology
Westminster Theological Seminary
Philadelphia, Pennsylvania

PRESBYTERIAN AND REFORMED PUBLISHING CO.
Phillipsburg, New Jersey

Library of Congress Cataloging in Publication Data

Murray, John, 1898-1975.
    Christian baptism.

    Originally published: Phillipsburg, N.J.:
Presbyterian and Reformed Pub. Co., 1980.
    Includes bibliographical references.
    1. Baptism. I. Title.
BV811.2.M87   1983   234'.161   83-4422

ISBN 0-87552-343-9 (pbk.)

Contents

Preface

In the course of the last three to four centuries it is questionable if any topic in Christian theology can claim as prolific a literary output as the subject of baptism. One reason for this lies at hand. It is the controversy occasioned by the anabaptist rejection of the catholic position and practice. It might seem presumptuous and superfluous to encumber the library of books and pamphlets on the subject of baptism with another study on this theme. But the writer has been constrained to feel that his venture is not a work of supererogation.

Within protestant circles there is at the present time a widespread loss of conviction regarding the propriety and preceptive necessity of infant baptism. Even when the practice still persists, oftentimes there is little more than sentiment and tradition behind it. Such a situation is deplorable. Traditional sentiment can never be pleaded as the proper ground for any element of the worship of the church of God. Divine institution is the only warrant. And when sentiment or custom takes the place of the recognition of divine prescription in any particular that concerns the elements of divine worship, a state of mind is revealed which is altogether alien to the nature of the church and of the worship which it offers to God.

Furthermore, among seriously minded evangelical Christians, whose background and tradition have not been by any means baptist, there is a prevalent doubt as to the Biblical warrant for infant baptism. In this state of mind they are readily susceptible to baptist influence both as respects the insistence upon immersion as the only valid mode and the rejection of infant baptism. The movement away from the established Churches and toward independency has given a great deal of momentum to the tendency to adopt baptistic tenets and practice without necessarily adopting a baptist denomination.

It is with the hope that this study may contribute towards the correction of such evils that it is being offered to the public. While the writer has particularly in view those who are on the margin of abandoning the position taken in this study and of embracing what is in practice, if not in theory, the baptist position, and while it is hoped that many such may be reclaimed to understand that immersion is not necessary to baptism and that infant baptism is the divine institution, yet it is also hoped that this humble attempt may also be instrumental in constraining even baptists to reconsider their position.

The writer knows only too well how persuasive the baptist argument respecting infant baptism can be made to appear and how conclusive it becomes to many earnest and sincere Christians. He knows also how difficult it is to persuade people, whose thinking has been moulded after the baptist pattern, that the argument for infant baptism is Scriptural. But the reason for this is that to think organically of the Scripture revelation is much more difficult than to think atomistically. The argument for infant baptism rests upon the recognition that God's redemptive action and revelation in this world are covenantal. In a word, redemptive action is covenant action and redemptive revelation is covenant revelation. Embedded in this covenantal action of God is the principle that the infant seed of believers are embraced with their parents in the covenant relation and provision. It is this method of God's administration of grace in the world that must be appreciated. It belongs to the New Testament as well as to the Old. It is its presence and significance that grounds infant baptism. And it is the perception of its significance that illumines for us the meaning of this ordinance.

There are certain viewpoints, or at least angles of thought, expressed and sometimes insisted upon which diverge from the judgment of some of the most respected of Reformed writers. In the footnotes I have discussed some of these divergences at greater length. But it did not appear to be in the best interests of the purpose in view to burden the argument proper by expanded discussion of several details. In reference to the argument for infant baptism, in particular, I have tried to emphasize those aspects of the question which call for greater emphasis and to give the presentation of the evidence a certain direction which, in my judgment, is better calculated to meet certain baptist objections. It has been my purpose to concentrate on what is basic and central, in the hope that the force of the evidence may not be dissipated by what is liable to be the consequence of more diffuse discussion. If these pages which follow minister to the conviction that the positions taken are grounded upon Scripture and enhance appreciation of the grace of God which the institution of baptism evinces, the author will be highly rewarded.

I

The Import of Baptism

The ordinance of baptism with which we are concerned is
the ordinance that was instituted by our Lord himself on the
eve of his ascension when he gave to his disciples the commission, "Go ye therefore and disciple all the nations, baptising
them in the name of the Father, and of the Son, and of the
Holy Spirit, teaching them to observe all things whatsoever
I have commanded you" (Matt. 28:19, 20). Other baptismal
rites had preceded this commission. There was the baptism
of John the Baptist. But John's baptism is not to be identified
with the ordinance instituted by Christ on the eve of his
ascension.[1] The character of John's baptism was analogous to

---

[1] *Cf. contra* John Calvin: *Institutes of the Christian Religion*, IV, xv, 7 and
18; IV, xvi, 27; John Gill: *A Complete Body of Doctrinal and Practical Di-
vinity* (London, 1796), Vol. III, pp. 290 f. Calvin maintains that the baptism of John and that dispensed by the apostles during the ministry of our
Lord on earth was the same as that enjoined by our Lord in the great
commission. He argues that the baptism of Matthew 28:19, 20 was not
the original institution of baptism. His interpretation of Acts 19:1-6 in
Inst. IV, xv, 18 does not appear to be a tenable one. The element of truth
in Calvin's contention for the identity of all three baptisms is sufficiently
guarded by the interpretation which the present writer presents above.
Cf. Edward Williams: *Antipaedobaptism Examined, Works* (London, 1862),
Vol. II, pp. 67 ff.; N. B. Stonehouse: "The Gift of the Holy Spirit" in
The Westminster Theological Journal, November, 1950 (Vol. XIII, No. 1),
p. 13, n. 12. Dr. Stonehouse takes the position that "specifically Christian
baptism began only with the establishment of the Christian church following the exaltation of Christ". He also thinks, however, that "the
baptism by the disciples of Jesus mentioned in John 4:1 ff. may best be
understood as a continuation of John's baptism". Although the question
as to whether the baptism by Jesus' disciples aligns itself more closely
with John's baptism rather than with Christian baptism is not of great
importance, I am disposed to think that the baptism by Jesus' disciples
points more in the direction of the significance of Christian baptism than
does the baptism of John. The reason for this judgment is given in the
next paragraph.

the character of his ministry. John prepared the way of the Lord and his ministry was preparatory, transitional, and introductive. So was his baptism. We may no more identify the baptism of John with the ordinance instituted by Christ than we may identify the ministry and mission of John with the ministry and mission of Christ. Hence we cannot derive from the nature of John's baptism the precise import of the ordinance of Christian baptism.

There was also the baptism that accompanied the ministry of Jesus prior to his death and resurrection (John 3:22, 26; 4:1, 2). These are the only references to this baptismal rite, which was actually performed not by Jesus himself but by his disciples (John 4:2). What its significance was it is difficult to say. We should be justified in inferring that it stood in a closer relationship to the ordinance instituted just before the ascension than did the baptism of John. It apparently indicated rather markedly the acceptance of Jesus as the Messiah and, in that sense, the discipleship of Jesus rather than that of John, a discipleship which John himself recognised as the only proper result of his own ministry and a discipleship urgently enjoined by John when he said, "He that hath the bride is the bridegroom: but the friend of the bridegroom, which standeth and heareth him, rejoiceth greatly because of the bridegroom's voice: this my joy therefore is fulfilled. He must increase, but I must decrease" (John 3:29, 30). Yet we do not have warrant by which to identify this baptism during Jesus' earthly ministry with the ordinance of Matthew 28:19, 20. The latter is baptism in the name of the Father, and of the Son, and of the Holy Ghost. We have no warrant to suppose that the earlier rite took this form. It is quite reasonable to believe that there was a very close relation between these two rites both in the mind of Jesus himself and in the recognition of the disciples. Indeed, so close may have been the relation that baptism in the name of the triune God was the necessary development of the earlier rite. But we are compelled to recognise the distinctiveness of the rite enunciated and embodied in the great commission. It is from the terms of this institution and from subsequent references in the New Testament that we are to derive the precise import of this ordinance.

We are liable to be misled by the nature of the ordinance, as one of washing with water, into thinking that the basic import is that of purification. However important that element is and even though it is included in the import of baptism, it does not appear to be the most central or basic element. We must take our point of departure from the very formula which Jesus used in the institution, "baptising them into the name of the Father, and of the Son, and of the Holy Spirit" (Matt. 28:19). It is this notion of "baptising into" that must be appreciated and analysed. This formula appears in other connections, as, for example, "baptised into Moses" (I Cor. 10:2) and "baptised into the name of Paul" (I Cor. 1:13). It is apparent that it expresses a relationship to the person into whom or into whose name persons may have been baptised. It is this fact of relationship that is basic. Hence we have to ask the question: what kind of relationship?

It is here that some of the most relevant references in the New Testament afford us light and direction. Such passages as Romans 6:3–6; I Corinthians 12:13; Galatians 3:27,28; Colossians 2:11, 12 plainly indicate that union with Christ is the governing idea. Baptism signifies union with Christ in his death, burial, and resurrection. It is because believers are united to Christ in the efficacy of his death, in the power of his resurrection, and in the fellowship of his grace that they are one body. They are united to Christ and therefore to one another. Of this union baptism is the sign and seal. The relationship which baptism signifies is therefore that of union, and union with Christ is its basic and central import.[2]

---

[2] The Westminster Confession of Faith and the Catechisms reflect a fine insight in this regard; *cf.* Confession of Faith, Chapter XXVIII, Section I; Larger Catechism, Question 165; Shorter Catechism, Question 94. The Shorter Catechism says with its characteristic brevity and clarity, "Baptism is a sacrament, wherein the washing with water, in the name of the Father, and of the Son, and of the Holy Ghost, doth signify and seal our ingrafting into Christ, and partaking of the benefits of the covenant of grace, and our engagement to be the Lord's". Calvin in his excellent discussion in *Inst.* IV, xv and xvi does not place this aspect of the import of baptism in the forefront but rather the purgation of sin in the blood of Christ and the mortification of the flesh in regeneration; *cf. Inst.* IV, xvi, 2. Yet this element is by no means absent. He lists it as the third advantage which our faith receives from baptism; *cf. Inst.* IV, xv, 1–6.

Pierre Ch. Marcel, most recently, in his able treatment of the subject of

We must bear in mind, however, that the formula which our Lord used in the institution of this ordinance is more inclusive than that of union with himself. Baptism is into the name of the Father, and of the Son, and of the Holy Ghost. It means therefore that a relation of union to the three persons of the Godhead is thereby signified. This is entirely consonant with the teaching of our Lord elsewhere regarding the union that is established by faith in him. It is not only union with himself but also with the Father and the Holy Spirit (*cf.* John 14:16, 17, 23; 17:21–23). Consequently baptism, by the very words of institution, signifies union with the Father and the Son and the Holy Ghost, and this means with the three persons of the trinity, both in the unity expressed by their joint possession of the one name and in the richness of the distinctive relationship which each person of the Godhead sustains to the people of God in the economy of the covenant of grace.

As was indicated above, we may not, however, exclude from the import of baptism the notion of purification. Baptism is dispensed by the application of water in a way that is expressive of cleansing. And it would be unreasonable to suppose that this action bears no analogy to that which is signified by it. There are two respects in which cleansing or purification takes place at the inception of the relationship which is signified and sealed by baptism, namely, purification from the defilement and purification from the guilt of sin.

There does not appear to be in the New Testament any passage which expressly says that baptism represents purification from the defilement of sin, that is to say, regeneration. But since baptism is washing with water, since it involves a religious use of water, and since regeneration is expressed elsewhere in terms of washing (John 3:5; Titus 3:5; I Cor. 6:11),

baptism says: "Le baptême représente, figure et signifie la purification; la cène représente, figure et signifie la nourriture spirituelle" (*La Revue Réformée*, Oct., 1950, "Le Baptême, Sacrement de L'Alliance de Grace", p. 21). Later on in this dissertation, however, Marcel develops quite fully the concept of union with Christ as the principal element in baptism (see pp. 106 ff.). He says: "Nous sommes vraiment incorporés au corps de Christ quand sa mort montre en nous son fruit. Cette communion, cette conformité en sa mort est l'élément principal du baptême, où nous est figuré non seulement notre purification, mais aussi notre mise à mort et la destruction du vieil homme" (*ibid.*, p. 109).

it is difficult, if not impossible, to escape the conclusion that this washing with water involved in baptism represents that indispensable purification which is presupposed in union with Christ and without which no one can enter into the kingdom of God. There is also the consideration that baptism is the circumcision of the New Testament (Col. 2:11, 12). Circumcision, without doubt, symbolised purification from defilement. We should infer that baptism does also.

In reference to the other respect in which purification applies to the import of baptism there need be no question: it represents purification from the guilt of sin. Earlier it was maintained that the baptism of John and Christian baptism must not be identified. It does not follow that there is no similarity in respect of import. Both rites involved washing with water and we must therefore discover some element that will apply to both. John's baptism did have reference to the forgiveness of sins (Matt. 3:6; Mark 1:4; Luke 3:3). We should expect that such a reference could not be excluded from the import of Christian baptism. Such an expectation is confirmed by express intimation in other passages; Christian baptism stands in a similar relation to the remission of sins (Acts 2:38; 22:16; I Pet. 3:21). We may therefore conclude that baptism represents the remission of sin or, in other words, purification from the guilt of sin by the sprinkling of the blood of Christ.

We may say then that baptism signifies union with Christ in the virtue of his death and the power of his resurrection, purification from the defilement of sin by the renewing grace of the Holy Spirit, and purification from the guilt of sin by the sprinkling of the blood of Christ. The emphasis must be placed, however, upon union with Christ. It is this that is central, and it is this notion that appears more explicitly and pervasively than any other. Hence our view of baptism must be governed by this concept. Anything less than that kind of union expressed in the formula of institution will provide too restricted a conception and will distort our view of what is exhibited and sealed by this ordinance.

II

The Mode of Baptism

Baptism signifies and seals union with Christ and cleansing from the pollution and guilt of sin. The central import is that of union with Christ, ingrafting into him, and partaking of the benefits of the covenant of grace. In reference to the mode of baptism the question is whether a particular method of applying water or of relating the person to water is of the essence of the symbolism.[3] The Baptist contention is that the mode is of the essence of the symbolism and that, since to baptise means to immerse, baptism is not properly administered by any other mode. The Baptist argument rests mainly upon two contentions: (1) that $\beta a\pi\tau i\zeta\omega$ means to immerse[4] and (2) that passages like Romans 6:3-6 and Colossians 2:11, 12 plainly imply that the death and resurrection of Christ provide us with the pattern for immersion in, and emergence from, the water.[5]

We may now proceed to examine these two arguments.

[3] *Cf.* James Bannerman: *The Church of Christ* (Edinburgh, 1868), Vol. II, p. 123.

[4] *Cf.* Alexander Carson: *Baptism in its Modes and Subjects* (Philadelphia, 1845), p. 19; A. H. Strong: *Systematic Theology* (Philadelphia, 1909), Vol. III, p. 993. Carson says, "BAPTO has two meanings; *baptizo* in the whole history of the Greek language has but one. It not only signifies to dip or immerse, but it never has any other meaning." Strong says, "This is immersion, and immersion only". *Cf.* also John Gill: *op. cit.*, pp. 307 ff.; Abraham Booth: *Paedobaptism Examined* (London, 1829), Vol. I, pp. 40-131.

[5] *Cf.* Alexander Carson: *op. cit.*, pp. 142 ff.; A. H. Strong: *op. cit.*, pp. 940 ff.; John Gill: *op. cit.*, p. 310; Abraham Booth: *op. cit.*, pp. 162 ff. For a statement and criticism of the Baptist position *cf.* Robert Wilson: *Infant Baptism a Scriptural Service, and Dipping Unnecessary to its Right Administration* (London, 1848), pp. 286 ff.

A. *The Meaning of* βαπτίζω

The Old Testament. In the Septuagint[6] βαπτίζω occurs very
infrequently (II Kings 5:14; Isa. 21:4). In Isaiah 21:4 it is
used in a figurative sense to translate the Hebrew word בעת
which means to terrify, startle, or fall upon. It would appear
that nothing very determinative regarding the precise import
of βαπτίζω can be derived from this instance. In II Kings
5:14 the reference is to Naaman's baptising of himself seven
times in Jordan, and βαπτίζω translates the Hebrew word
טבל. It is the word βάπτω which occurs most frequently in
the Septuagint, occurring some seventeen times. In most of
these instances it translates the Hebrew word טבל just as
βαπτίζω does in II Kings 5:14. טבל means to dip or be moist
with. In Leviticus 11:32 βάπτω translates the Hebrew word
בוא and no doubt refers to immersion — the articles concerned
are put into water. In Psalm 68:23(24) βάπτω translates the
Hebrew word מחץ which means to smite through. But the
Greek seems to convey a different idea, one akin to that of
the Hebrew word טבל.

There need be no question then that טבל means to dip
and so also does βάπτω which is the Greek rendering.
Furthermore, that βάπτω may also sometimes refer to immersion there need be no question. This appears in Leviticus
11:32. The question is whether טבל and βάπτω *necessarily*
refer to immersion and that they therefore mean to immerse.
It can readily be shown that טבל and βάπτω do not *mean*
immersion. That is to say, the dipping denoted by טבל and

[6] In the discussion which follows account is taken simply of instances
appearing in the canonical books of the Old Testament. Furthermore, it
is not deemed necessary to enter into a detailed discussion of each instance
of βάπτω and βαπτίζω. The purpose of our discussion is simply to show
that βάπτω in the usage of the LXX does not mean immersion and that
it cannot be shown that βαπτίζω means immersion. It is not forgotten,
of course, that as able an immersionist as Alexander Carson allows that
βάπτω does not always mean to dip but that it also has a secondary and
derived meaning, namely, to dye (*cf. op. cit.*, pp. 18 ff.). Other immersionists, however, do not concede as much as Carson. In any case it is well to
review the Old Testament usage in reference to βάπτω. This provides a
necessary and suitable introduction to the New Testament usage in reference to βαπτίζω and its cognates. For discussion of Isaiah 21:4 *cf.* Robert
Wilson: *op. cit.*, pp. 178 f., 267 ff.

βάπτω is not always to be equated with immersion. This fact that dipping is not equivalent to immersion needs to be stressed at the outset. Far too often in anti-baptist discussions this fact is overlooked and a good deal of unnecessary argumentation arises from the oversight.

In Leviticus 14:6, 51 we have the ritual prescribed for the cleansing of a leper and of a house in which the plague of leprosy appeared. The priest was to take the cedar wood and the scarlet and the hyssop and the living bird and dip them in the blood of the bird that was slain. It is obvious that a living bird cannot be immersed in the blood of another bird. It may be dipped in such blood but such dipping could not be immersion. Here is a case where βάπτω is used to denote an action that cannot be construed as immersion. And so βάπτω does not *mean* immersion. It can refer to an action performed by immersion but it can also refer to an action that does not involve immersion at all. Hence there is no reason arising from the meaning of the word βάπτω why in any instance of its occurrence it should refer to immersion. When it does refer to immersion our knowledge that this is the case is not derived from the word βάπτω but from other considerations.

It is also worthy of note that in these two instances the live bird was to be baptised *into the blood* (εἰς τὸ αἷμα) of the slain bird. Hence even "baptism into" (βάπτω εἰς) does not mean to immerse, and the preposition "into" does not_ add any force to the argument that βάπτω *means* to immerse.[6a]

[6a] An objection to the validity of the argument drawn from Leviticus 14:6,51 could be urged on the basis of the consideration that the blood of the bird that was slain flowed into the living water in the earthenware vessel and that it was not simply in the blood of the slain bird that the living bird, the cedar wood, the scarlet, and the hyssop were dipped but in the mixture of water and blood in the earthenware vessel. This is the view of able commentators such as Keil and Delitzsch, S. H. Kellogg, J. P. Lange and others. If this view of the ritual could be proven, the position taken above would have to be modified. For it might be maintained that, in such a case, there could be enough fluid for immersion of the four items specified. There are, however, two things to be said in reference to this objection. (1) Even on the supposition that it was in a mixture of blood and water that the items were dipped, it is not apparent that there would have been enough fluid for purposes of immersion. (2) The terms of the passage do not indicate that the procedure

In Leviticus 14:16 we have another instance which, while not as conclusive as Leviticus 14:6, 51, nevertheless, points in the same direction. This has reference to the sprinkling of oil. The priest took some of the log of oil and poured it into the palm of his left hand. Then he dipped his right finger in the oil that was in the palm of his left hand and sprinkled the oil seven times before the Lord. Now it *may* be possible to pour into the cupped left hand enough oil so that the right finger may be immersed in this oil. But it is not an easy performance. The passage concerned does not indicate any such requirement. All that is prescribed is dipping of the right finger in the oil which is in the palm of the left hand, and it is quite unreasonable to suppose that immersion of that right finger was required. Dipping of the right finger in the oil was all that was requisite for the sprinkling which followed, and dipping without the necessity of immersion is rather plainly indicated to be the action in view.

Again in Ruth 2:14 we have the word of Boaz to Ruth: "dip thy morsel in the vinegar". It would be quite unreasonable to insist that the custom to which Boaz referred

was such as is supposed in this objection. Leviticus 14:6 says simply that the four items were dipped "in the blood of the bird that had been slain upon the living water". And in Leviticus 14:51,52 the blood of the bird that had been slain and the living water are distinguished. In verse 51 it is distinctly specified that the four items were to be dipped "in the blood of the slain bird, and in the living water". Verse 52, again, distinguishes between the blood of the slain bird and the living water, just as it distinguishes between the living bird and the other three items. "And he shall cleanse the house with the blood of the bird, and with the living water, and with the living bird, and with the cedar-wood, and with the hyssop, and with the scarlet." Hence there does not appear to be good reason for adopting the view that it was in a mixture of blood and water that the items concerned were dipped nor good reason for relinquishing the view adopted.

If the Talmud should be appealed to in support of the view that the blood and the living water were mixed (see tractate *Negaim*, Chapter XIV, Mishnah 1), it should be borne in mind that the tradition referred to in this tractate distinctly provided that only a quarter of a log of living water was put in the earthenware vessel. Obviously a quarter of a log of water, together with the blood of the slain bird, would not provide enough fluid for immersion of the living bird, not to speak of the additional items which were to be dipped.

was to *immerse* one's morsel in the vinegar. On the other hand the idea of dipping something in vinegar is reasonable and natural. No doubt that was what Boaz had in mind.

This same meaning of βάπτω could also apply in I Samuel 14:27, where we are told that Jonathan put forth the end of the rod that was in his hand and dipped it in the honey. In this case it is of course not unreasonable to suppose that the end of the rod was completely covered by the honey. But it is not necessary to suppose this.

What we have found is this: there is one case where βάπτω and even βάπτω εἰς does not mean and cannot mean immersion (Lev. 14:6, 51); there is the other case where it is unreasonable to suppose that immersion was required or took place (Lev. 14:16); there is still another instance where dipping but not immersion is the reasonable and natural supposition (Ruth 2:14); finally, in the case of I Samuel 14:27 immersion is not unreasonable but it is not by any means necessary to the action denoted. Hence we have no reason to suppose that in a great many other instances immersion is the action denoted by βάπτω. In other words, we have no ground upon which to insist that in Exodus 12:22; Leviticus 4:6, 17; 9:9; Numbers 19:18; Deuteronomy 33:24; II Kings 8:15 immersion is the mode of action referred to in the respective cases. There is nothing in the Hebrew word used nor in the context of the passages concerned which requires immersion. And the Greek word βάπτω, as we have just found, does not require immersion. So we are compelled to conclude that there is nothing to show that in any of these instances just cited immersion was practised or even suggested. And returning to II Kings 5:14, the case of Naaman, where we have βαπτίζω rather than βάπτω, this instance cannot be adduced to prove that Naaman immersed himself in Jordan. Without doubt he bathed himself in Jordan; but there is no evidence derived from the terms used either in Hebrew or Greek, or from the details of the narrative, to prove that Naaman immersed himself. Again, Joshua 3:15 cannot be adduced to prove that the priests' feet were immersed in Jordan. We are told that their feet were baptised in the brink of the river. It is quite possible that their feet were immersed in the water. But there is nothing to prove this. Dipping of their feet in the brink of the river is all that is necessary to satisfy the terms used both in Hebrew and Greek. Besides, in verse 13 we are told that, when the *soles* of the feet of the priests would rest in Jordan, the waters would be cut off and stand in one heap. In verses 15 and 16 we are told that, when the feet of the priests were *dipped* in the brink of the river, the waters stood and rose up in one heap. Surely the kind of contact with the water, mentioned in verse 13, satisfies the terms of verse 15. To demand more for dipping than the resting of the soles of the priests' feet in the water would be indefensible.

In all of the passages so far considered there is only one instance where βάπτω clearly refers to an action which involved immersion. It is the case of Leviticus 11:32. It is also highly probable that in Job 9:31 the idea corresponds to that of immersion. At least the idea is much stronger than that of mere dipping and is more akin to that of plunging. Only in these two passages is the idea of immersion required to express the action denoted by βάπτω.

There are still two passages to be considered: Daniel 4:30 (LXX vs. 33); 5:21. In these instances βάπτω translates the Aramaic verb צבע. This Aramaic verb occurs elsewhere in the book of Daniel (*cf.* 4:12, 20, 22). But only in 4:30; 5:21 is it translated by the Greek verb βάπτω. The Septuagint rendering of the clause in question in each case is: καὶ ἀπὸ τῆς δρόσου τοῦ οὐρανοῦ τὸ σῶμα αὐτοῦ ἐβάφη. This refers to Nebuchadnezzar whose body was bathed with the dew of heaven. It is possible that the meaning of the Greek rendering is that his body was dipped in the dew of heaven, that is to say, dipped in the dew with which the herbs and grass of the field were drenched. It may be that the thought expressed is that his body was drenched or bathed from the dew of heaven. On the other hand, the meaning may be as weak as that his body was simply moist or wet with the dew of heaven. In any case the thought cannot be adjusted to the notion that his body was immersed in the dew of heaven. This would require the most arbitrary and unnatural twisting of the terms and would amount to unreason in the lowest degree. So again we have an instance of the use of βάπτω in another sense than that of immersion. Therefore it does not mean immersion.

The New Testament. In the usage of the New Testament βάπτω recedes into the background and βαπτίζω comes into the foreground. The former occurs only four times (Luke 16:24; John 13:26(2); Rev. 19:13) whereas the latter seventy five to eighty times. There are twenty occurrences of the substantive βάπτισμα and three of βαπτισμός.

In determining the meaning of these terms used to denote baptism it must be remembered again that the question is not whether they may be used to denote an action performed by immersion. It is not our interest to deny that they may be used to denote such an action. The question is whether these terms *mean* immersion and therefore always imply in one way or another the act of immersion and could not properly denote an action performed by any other mode. This is the precise question that is relevant to the Baptist contention. And we are concerned now to deal with the evidence which the New Testament itself presents. The thesis which we are propounding is that the terms for baptism are used to denote actions which were not performed by the mode of immersion and that, while these terms could refer to immersion, yet they do not *mean* immersion. In other words, we undertake to show that the Baptist contention that βαπτίζω and its cognates mean immersion is not borne out by the evidence and that βαπτίζω can be used to denote an action which neither indicates nor implies immersion. We propose to show this by appeal to several passages and groups of passages.

1. *Matthew 15:2; Mark 7:2–5; Luke 11:38.*

In Matthew 15:2; Mark 7:2–5 we have express allusion to the custom of the Jews, called "the tradition of the elders", to wash their hands before eating bread. "Why do thy disciples transgress the tradition of the elders? For they do not wash their hands when they eat bread" (Matt. 15:2). "For the Pharisees and all the Jews, except they wash their hands, do not eat, holding the tradition of the elders" (Mark 7:3). There is some uncertainty as to the precise force of the word πυγμή in the clause, ἐὰν μὴ πυγμῇ νίψωνται τὰς χεῖρας, whether it refers to the wrist or to the fist. Both Lightfoot and Edersheim claim that according to Jewish custom there were two ways of washing the hands before eating, namely, by dipping the hands in water or by pouring water over the hands. In the former case πυγμή may refer to the washing of one hand with the cupped fist of the other. In the latter case there is every good reason for believing that πυγμή refers to the wrist. It is distinctly provided in the Talmudic tractate *Yadayim* that water was to be poured over the hands to the wrist. Chapter II, Mishnah 3, reads as follows: "Hands become unclean and are made clean as far as the wrist. How so? If he poured the first water over the hands as far as the wrist and poured the second water over the hands beyond the wrist and the latter flowed back to the hands, the hands nevertheless become clean."[7] It would appear that Edersheim is correct when he says, "Accordingly, the words of St. Mark can only mean that the Pharisees eat not 'except they wash their hands to the wrist' ".[8] In any case it is a washing of the hands that is in view and, most probably, washing of the hands up to the wrist.

In Luke 11:38 this same tradition is referred to when we are told that the Pharisee marvelled because Jesus "had not first baptised himself before dinner" (οὐ πρῶτον ἐβαπτίσθη πρὸ τοῦ ἀρίστου). There is no reason to suppose that anything else than the tradition referred to above is in view here, and everything would point to that conclusion. The important observation now is that this tradition is decribed as baptising oneself (for this is the force of the form ἐβαπτίσθη)

---

[7] *The Babylonian Talmud: Seder Tohoroth* (London, The Soncino Press, 1948), p. 552; *cf.* Alfred Edersheim: *The Life and Times of Jesus the Messiah* (New York, 1910), Vol. II, pp. 10 ff.; John Lightfoot: *Works* (ed. Pitman, London, 1823), Vol. IX, p. 153, Vol. XI, pp. 399 ff.; H. B. Swete: *Com. ad loc.*; Joseph Addison Alexander: *Com. ad loc.*

In appealing to the Talmud caution has to be exercised. The committal to writing of a great many of these traditions is later than the early Christian era. There is often doubt as to the antiquity of some of these traditions, and so in many cases we cannot be sure that they go back as far as the first century of the Christian era. However, the rabbinic tradition embodied in the Talmud in many instances antedates the Christian era and we can discover in the Talmud that which exactly corresponds to the traditions so frequently condemned by our Lord. Hence there is oftentimes a great deal of help derived from the Talmud in the interpretation of the New Testament.

[8] *Op. cit.* p. 11.

and provides evidence that βαπτίζω can be used with reference
to an action which did not involve immersing oneself. Washing the hands by dipping them in water or, more probably, by
pouring water upon them can be called baptism.

It is quite unwarranted to insist that on this occasion (Luke
11:38) there must be allusion to the Jewish practice of immersion and that what the Pharisee expected on this occasion was
that Jesus should have plunged himself in water. There is no
evidence to support such a supposition and the evidence is
decidedly against it. Jewish tradition, it is true, did prescribe
immersion in certain cases of uncleanness. *Seder Tohoroth* in
the Babylonian Talmud includes several tractates which
evince these prescriptions, and the tractate *Mikwaoth* deals
expressly with the bathing-pool which served these purposes.[9]
In this bathing-pool persons as well as vessels and other articles were immersed. But rabbinic tradition prescribed immersion not for the washing and purification which preceded
eating, as in this case, but for the uncleanness contracted by
such things as leprosy and various kinds of running issue.[10]
These tractates deal with the way in which such uncleanness
was to be removed. There is no evidence that the Pharisee,
in the instance of Luke 11:38, would or could have considered
Jesus as having contracted such defilement as, in accordance

---

[9] *The Babylonian Talmud*: *Seder Tohoroth* (as cited), pp. 419 ff.

[10] *Cf.* the Talmudic tractate *Kelim*, Chapter I, Mishnah 5 (*The Babylonian Talmud* as cited, pp. 9 f.); the Talmudic tractate *Negaim*, Chapter
XIV, Mishnah 2, 3, 8 (*The Babylonian Talmud* as cited, pp. 292 ff.). It is
noteworthy in this connection that the Old Testament prescriptions for
the cleansing of uncleanness arising from leprosy or a running issue or the
seed of copulation *etc.* do not stipulate that the bathing required be by
immersion. It was distinctly prescribed that the person to be cleansed
should bathe himself in water. Sometimes the expression used is that he
bathe his flesh in water and on at least one occasion it is said that he must
bathe *all* his flesh in water (Lev. 15:16). But the terms used for such
bathing are not such as to require immersion. In Hebrew the term is רחץ
and in the LXX λούω (*cf.* Lev. 14:8, 9; 15:1–33). It may be that in many
cases the bathing was performed by immersion. But this was not stipulated
and there were many circumstances under which it would be most difficult,
if not impossible, for immersion to take place (*cf.* especially Lev. 15:13).
The important consideration is that immersion was not prescribed (*cf.* for
a discussion of Mosaic purifications Edward Beecher: *Baptism in reference
to its Import and Modes*, New York, 1849, pp. 32 ff.).

with rabbinic prescription and tradition, required immersion for purification. In other words, there is no evidence which would indicate that the Pharisee expected of Jesus anything more than the washing referred to in Matthew 15:2; Mark 7:3, a washing of the hands as far as the wrist, either by pouring water over them or by dipping them in water. The significant fact is that such washing is referred to as baptising oneself.

These passages offer another relevant datum. It concerns Mark 7:4, and is to the effect that the Jews on returning from the market-place do not eat except they wash themselves. Some question has been raised as to whether this refers to the purifying of their own bodies or to the purifying of the food brought from the market. While it might not be impossible for the form in which the verb appears to bear this latter sense yet the terms used do not suggest it and the context provides strong presumption against it. The preceding verse refers to the washing of the hands before eating and verse 5 brings us back to the same tradition in the question addressed by the Pharisees and Scribes: "Why do thy disciples walk contrary to the tradition of the elders, but eat bread with defiled hands?". It would be natural to relate the statement of verse 4 — "and when they come from the market-place they do not eat except they wash" — to the precise tradition mentioned in verses 3 and 5.

An observation to which interest and importance attach is that there is a variant in the manuscript authority. Some manuscripts use the word $\beta\alpha\pi\tau\iota\zeta\omega$ in verse 4, others the word $\dot{\rho}\alpha\nu\tau\iota\zeta\omega$. The latter means to sprinkle, and so the rendering in this case would be: "and when they come from the market-place they do not eat except they sprinkle themselves". If this reading is correct then this passage offers proof that sprinkling was regarded by the Jews as a proper mode for the removal of defilement. We should have to suppose that the intercourse of the market-place was regarded by the Jews as increasing the defilement and it would be reasonable to think that the purification required for this defilement would be more elaborate or extensive than that which was ordinarily necessary before eating, that is to say, more extensive than the mere washing of the hands. The reading "to sprinkle" would very readily supply the answer to this more extensive purification.

If we were to adopt the reading which uses the word βαπτίζω, this might appear to give support to the Baptist contention that immersion is the practice alluded to. In other words, it may be argued that while, ordinarily, all that is requisite before eating is the washing of the hands yet after the intercourse of the market-place the total washing of immersion is requisite. And it could be argued that this is the force of the distinction made between the requisition referred to in verse 3 and that referred to in verse 4. Additional support might be derived from the consideration that in the latter part of verse 4 the "baptism of cups and pots and brazen vessels" are adduced as examples of the traditions in view, baptisms which were presumptively performed by immersion.[11]

There is no good reason for controverting the validity of this argument provided evidence could be adduced to prove that after return from the market-place rabbinic or Pharisaic tradition required immersion before eating. In that event this

[11] There is good reason to believe that the "baptisms of cups and pots and brasen vessels", referred to in Mark 7:4, refer to immersion (cf. the Talmudic tractate *Kelim*, Chapter XXV, Mishnah 3, 5). The reference to the baptism of "couches" (κλινῶν) does not appear in several manuscripts. Hence the text is in question. There need be no question, however, that the Jews did require the purification of couches and beds (cf. Lev. 15:20). Edward Beecher, for example, does not appear to be on stable ground when he says, "But above all, the immersion of the couches on which they reclined at meals is out of the question" (op. cit., p. 39; cf. Robert Wilson: op. cit., pp. 229 f.). Apart from the question as to whether or not the reference in this case is to the immersion of couches (even assuming that the text is correct), Beecher's flat denial of the possibility of a reference to immersion does not appear to be warranted. The Talmudic tractate *Kelim*, again, indicates that in rabbinic tradition provision was made that beds might be purified in parts and even for the dismantling of beds in order to purification by immersion (see Chapter XVIII, Mishnah 9; Chapter XIX, Mishnah 1. The relevant words in the latter are, "If a man dismantled a bed in order that he might immerse it . . ."). Alexander Carson, without appealing to these rabbinic provisions and without appeal to the Talmud, observes with good warrant: "the couches might have been so constructed, that they might be conveniently taken to pieces, for the purpose of purification" (op. cit., p. 76). It is not now being contended, of course, that the baptism of couches necessarily refers to immersion. All that is being maintained is that we are not justified in appealing to Mark 7:4b to show that βαπτισμός cannot here imply immersion. For diversity of mode in Levitical prescription cf. Robert Wilson: op. cit., pp. 228 f.

would be a case in which the word βαπτίζω would be used with reference to an action that was performed by immersion. We are not in the least concerned to deny that βαπτίζω can be thus used any more than are we interested in denying that in the latter part of verse 4 the word βαπτισμός is used with reference to actions which were performed by the mode of immersion. In other words, let us grant to the fullest extent that in verse 4 the verb βαπτίζω and the noun βαπτισμός are used with reference to acts of immersion, this by no means proves that either the verb or the noun *means* immersion in such a way that neither of them could be used with reference to an action performed by another mode. To adduce cases in which "baptise" or "baptism" is used to denote an action performed by immersion does not prove that they *mean* immersion. Our inquiry now is conducted to the end of showing simply that "to baptise" does not *mean* "to immerse".

There are, however, two premises upon which rests the argument that in verse 4a we have an instance of the use of βαπτίζω to denote an action performed by immersion: (1) that βαπτίζω is the proper reading; (2) that there is good evidence that on returning from the market-place immersion was the rabbinic requisition. Neither of these premises is substantiated. To say the least, there is doubt as to both. Hence the argument is not established. And it must be remembered that in Luke 11:38 we have an instance of the use of βαπτίζω with reference to an act of washing or cleansing which, in accordance with Matthew 15:2 and Mark 7:3, was performed by washing the hands. So there is no proof that in Mark 7:4a the word βαπτίζω is used in the sense of immersion.

2. *Hebrews 9:10–23.*

In verse 10 we have the expression "divers baptisms" (διαφόροις βαπτισμοῖς). The allusion is to various symbolical lustrations of the Old Testament. The word "divers" indicates that lustratory rites of various kinds are in view. It is not probable, however, that all the lustratory rites are contemplated. It is likely that those which had more direct relevance to the purification of persons are intended; the preceding verse, which is closely coordinated with verse 10, is concerned with the gifts and sacrifices which could not make him that performed the service perfect as to the conscience. But even if we recognise this delimitation we have still to note that lustrations of various kinds are envisaged.

The significance of this passage as it bears upon our present interest is that the "divers baptisms" referred to in verse 10 must surely include the lustrations expressly referred to in the succeeding verses. In these verses a contrast is drawn between the intrinsic inefficacy, or at least relative inefficacy, of the ritual ordinances of the Levitical economy and the transcendent efficacy and perfection of Christ's purificatory and expiatory work. In a word, the imperfection of the Levitical lustrations is contrasted with the lustration once for all perfected by Christ. In this sustained contrast every lustratory rite that comes within the writer's purview must be included in the "divers baptisms" of verse 10. And that simply means that the lustratory rites mentioned in the succeeding context must come within the scope of the "divers baptisms".

In verse 13 one of these lustratory ordinances is expressly stated to have been performed by sprinkling — "for if the blood of goats and bulls and ashes of an heifer sprinkling the unclean sanctifieth to the purifying of the flesh". When we bear in mind that here a lustratory rite of the old economy is contrasted in respect of its efficacy with the finality and perfection of the blood of Christ and when we remember that it was precisely this thought of relative inefficacy that prompted the reference to "divers baptisms", it becomes exegetically impossible to exclude this rite, or these rites, of verse 13 from the scope of the "divers baptisms". And this means that a lustratory rite performed by sprinkling can be called a baptism.

Again in verse 19 reference is made to the *sprinkling* of the book and all the people, and in verse 21 to the *sprinkling* of the tabernacle and all the vessels of the ministry (*cf*. Exod. 24:6–8). These ordinances are expressly stated in verse 23 to have been purificatory. We cannot exclude them from the scope of the "divers baptisms" of verse 10.

We must conclude, therefore, that the word "baptism" refers to an action that can be performed by sprinkling as well as by any other mode. It cannot, therefore, mean immersion.

Besides, we know that several of the Levitical lustrations, in addition to those mentioned in this chapter, were performed by sprinkling (*cf.* Lev. 14:4–7, 16, 49–53, 16:19; Numb. 8:5–7; 19:18, 19).[12] If the Baptist argument is valid then the "divers baptisms" of Hebrews 9:10 will have to be restricted to those lustratory rites which were performed by immersion and must exclude the most significant lustratory rites and actions of the old economy. On the face of it such a supposition is arbitrary. When examined it becomes quite untenable. For what lustratory rites are more pertinent to the contrast instituted than those which were performed by other modes than that of immersion, examples of which are given in the succeeding context? And what immersions,[13] prescribed in the Old Testament, are directly pertinent to the precise thought of this passage and will satisfy the description, "divers baptisms"?

This passage, therefore, provides us with an instance of the use of the word "baptism" ($\beta\alpha\pi\tau\iota\sigma\mu\delta\varsigma$) to denote actions which do not involve immersion. Baptism does not mean immersion but can refer to actions performed by other modes. This is what we might expect to be the case in such a passage as Hebrews 9:10. As we think of the diverse modes of cleansing in the Old Testament, sprinkling stands out most promi-

---

[12] There are so many instances of sprinkling in the ritual of the Mosaic economy that it is not necessary to give the citations. In connection with the blood of the sacrifices no action of the priest was more prominent than the sprinkling of the blood. And the significance of sprinkling is shown by nothing more than by the fact that when the high priest went into the holiest of all once a year on the great day of atonement he sprinkled the blood of the sin-offerings seven times before the mercy-seat and upon the mercy-seat (Lev. 16:14, 15). That this sprinkling had reference to cleansing appears from Leviticus 16:19: "And he shall sprinkle with the blood upon it (the altar) with his finger seven times, and cleanse it, and hallow it from the uncleannesses of the children of Israel". The Hebrew words used for the act of sprinkling are זרק and נזה. Ezekiel 36:25 indicates as clearly as any text in the Old Testament the purificatory significance of sprinkling and the adequacy of sprinkling as a mode of purification. "Then will I sprinkle clean water upon you, and ye shall be clean: from all your filthiness, and from all your idols, will I cleanse you."

For a discussion of Hebrews 9:10 *cf.* Robert Wilson: *op. cit.*, pp. 214 ff.; Edward Beecher: op. cit., pp. 325 ff.

[13] This is a cogent question. It is difficult to know what immersions of the Levitical economy could be adduced to meet the requirements of this passage.

nently as one of the modes and appears in some of the most distinctive lustratory rites. It would be strange indeed if such rites were not in view in the expression, "divers baptisms".

3. *The Baptism of the Spirit.*

John the Baptist contrasted his own baptism with water with the baptism which Jesus was to dispense: "I indeed baptise you with water unto repentance . . . He shall baptise you with the Holy Spirit and fire" (Matt. 3:11; *cf.* Mark 1:8; Luke 3:16). Without question there is here an express allusion to Pentecost. Acts 1:5 and 11:16 confirm this, for in these passages the contrast between John's baptism and that of Jesus is instituted in connection with Pentecost: "John indeed baptised with water, but ye shall be baptised with the Holy Spirit not many days hence" (Acts 1:5). The coming of the Holy Spirit upon the disciples at Pentecost was undoubtedly baptism with the Holy Spirit and fire.

If baptism means immersion then the statement of John that Jesus would baptise with the Holy Spirit and fire must mean strictly "he shall immerse in the Holy Spirit and fire", and any language used with reference to the baptism of the Spirit, however figurative it may be, cannot depart from or violate this basic meaning. In other words, the symbolism cannot represent an entirely diverse mode of the relation of the disciples to the Holy Spirit and of the Holy Spirit to them.

But what we actually find is that the baptism of the Spirit is referred to in terms that are quite contrary to the idea of immersion and in fact preclude it. In Acts 1:8 the Holy Spirit is represented as coming upon the disciples: "Ye shall receive power after that the Holy Spirit has come upon you". The verb is ἐπέρχομαι and conveys the notion of "coming down upon". In Acts 2:17, 33 the Holy Spirit is represented as having been poured out, and the verb is ἐκχέω.[14] In Acts 10:44; 11:15 the Holy Spirit is represented as having fallen upon the persons concerned, and the verb is ἐπιπίπτω.

It is surely significant that the terms in each case are those

---

[14] *Cf.*, also, Titus 3:6 where the Holy Spirit as the Spirit of regeneration and renewal is said to have been "poured out" on us richly.

of affusion and not of immersion. Yet it is precisely this affusion that is called the baptism of the Holy Spirit.

Furthermore, the baptism with fire, referred to in the texts cited above, received its symbolic fulfilment, to say the least, in the cloven tongues like as of fire that sat upon the disciples at Pentecost (καὶ ἐκάθισεν ἐφ' ἕνα ἕκαστον αὐτῶν). If this is baptism with fire or, at least, the external symbol and sign of the baptism with fire, this baptism cannot be adjusted to the notion of immersion. But to the notion of immersion this phenomenon must be adjusted if the Baptist argument is correct that baptism means immersion.

It is not without relevance in this same connection that in the Old Testament the giving of the Spirit, in some cases explicitly referring to Pentecost, is promised in terms of pouring out, shedding forth, and sprinkling (Isa. 32:15; Joel 2:28; Prov. 1:23; Ezek. 36:25–27 where the Hebrew words are עָרָה, שָׁפַךְ and זָרַק meaning respectively to pour out, shed forth, and sprinkle). The language of the Old Testament provides the imagery of the New Testament and is quite foreign to the notion of immersion.

4. *The Sprinkling of the Blood of Christ.*

Baptism symbolises, represents, and seals the application to us of the blood of Christ for the removal of the guilt of sin. The figure used in the New Testament for this application of the blood of Christ is that of sprinkling (Hebrews 9:13, 14, 22; 10:22; 12:24; I Pet. 1:2). It would be strange if the baptism with water which represents the sprinkling of the blood of Christ could not properly and most significantly be performed by sprinkling. It cannot be too frequently insisted that according to Scripture cleansing from the guilt of sin is adequately and effectively administered by the mode of sprinkling no less than by the modes of affusion and immersion.[15]

Sufficient evidence has been presented to show that in the usage of the New Testament βαπτίζω does not mean to immerse. It can be used with reference to immersion but it can

---

[15] *Cf.* the discussion of Hebrews 9:10 above and particularly footnote 12.

also be used with reference to affusion and sprinkling. The New Testament, therefore, confirms the conclusions derived from the study of the Old Testament. Both Testaments mutually support each other in this respect.

It is, however, necessary to consider several other passages in the New Testament because they have been appealed to on both sides of the argument; some of them have been used by anti-immersionists and some by immersionists. It is necessary to examine them in order to determine whether they lend any weight to the argument in favour of or against the immersionist contention.

(a) *I Corinthians 10:2*. "All were baptised unto Moses in the cloud and in the sea." If the Baptist argument is correct, then there must be allusion to the mode of baptism in this text. At least, in order to satisfy the terms of the passage the children of Israel would have to be regarded as having been immersed in the cloud and in the sea.[16] Now it is only too apparent that they were not immersed in the sea — they passed through the sea upon dry ground. They did not enter into the water nor did the water come upon them (*cf*. Exod. 14:22). And as respects the cloud the reference is surely to the pillar of cloud that went before the children of Israel by day, a cloud that did not come upon them and into which they did not enter (*cf*. Exod. 13:21). So the word $\beta\alpha\pi\tau i\zeta\omega$ is used here with reference to an event or series of events which did not involve immersion in any way.

If the Baptist should retort that, since the children of Israel went into the midst of the sea (Exod. 14:22), were thus below the level of the water and hemmed in by it on both sides, they could be regarded as immersed in the sea, then we have the strange notion that to be below the level of the water amounts to immersion, even though the water comes into no contact whatsoever with our bodies. If this is the case, we shall have to revise our concept of

[16] John Gill says with reference to this passage that it was "a figure of baptism by immersion; as the Israelites were under the cloud, and so under water, and covered with it, as persons baptized by immersion are; and passed through the sea, that standing up as a wall on both sides them, with the cloud over them; thus surrounded they were as persons immersed in water, and so said to be baptized" (*op. cit.*, p. 311).

immersion to such an extent that it will be very different from that which is required by the Baptist contention. Besides, even if it were allowed that the going into the midst of the sea conforms to the idea of immersion, we must also take into account the cloud in which the children of Israel were baptised. There is no evidence that the children of Israel entered into the cloud or that the cloud came upon them. The main relevance of this passage is simply that the word βαπτίζω can be used without any intimation or suggestion of mode, that βαπτίζω itself does not express mode, and, particularly, that it does not mean to immerse.

(b) *Acts 8:26-40*. Anti-immersionists have appealed to this text in support of their own contention. They argue that since this was desert it would be improbable, if not impossible, to find enough water for purposes of immersion. This is not a valid argument. There is the possibility of sufficient water for such a purpose and the terms used would indicate that there was a well or pool or stream of water. Anti-immersionists cannot prove that there was not sufficient water for immersion. Neither can it be proved that the Ethiopian eunuch was not immersed by Philip.

It becomes equally necessary, however, to show that the Baptist appeal to this text to prove immersion is indefensible.[17] The text does not prove that Philip immersed the eunuch. Such an inference may seem to be contradicted by the express terms of the passage. Is it not said that both Philip and the eunuch went down into the water (καὶ κατέβησαν ἀμφότεροι εἰς τὸ ὕδωρ) and that they came up out of the water (ἀνέβησαν ἐκ τοῦ ὕδατος)? Is not immersion implied in the prepositions "into" and "out of"? The fact is that immersion cannot be established by such expressions. It should be noted that Philip as well as the eunuch went down into the water and came up out of the water. If such expressions imply or prove immersion, then they mean that Philip immersed himself as well as the eunuch. But such a supposition is quite unreason-

---

[17] *Cf.* John Gill: *op. cit.*, p. 309. Calvin, whom Gill quotes at this point says with reference to Acts 8:38: "Here we see what was the manner of baptising among the ancients, for they plunged the whole body into the water: now the use is, that the minister only sprinkles the body or the head".

able. Why should Philip have immersed himself, and why would Luke be so anxious to inform us that Philip immersed himself as well as the eunuch? It is not now maintained that Philip did not immerse the eunuch when he baptised him. That may have been the mode in this case. But what is to be recognised is — a fact too frequently ignored in the Baptist argumentation — that this passage does not prove immersion. The expressions, "they both went down into the water" and "they came up out of the water" are satisfied by the thought that they both went down to the water, stood on the brink or stepped into the edge, and that Philip baptised the eunuch by scooping up the water and pouring it or sprinkling it on him. This is *all* that can be shown to have occurred. As far as the going into, and coming up out of, the water are concerned nothing is stated in respect of the eunuch that is not also in respect of Philip himself. Hence there is no proof of immersion in this passage. What the actual mode was we simply do not know, and this text does not support the Baptist contention.

(c) *The Baptism of John.* The baptism of John is said to have been in Jordan (ἐν τῷ ʼΙορδάνῃ ποταμῷ — Matt. 3:6; Mark 1:5) and into Jordan (εἰς τὸν ʼΙορδάνην — Mark 1:9). He also baptised in Ainon near to Salim because there was much water there (ὕδατα πολλὰ ἦν ἐκεῖ — John 3:23).

At the outset it should be understood that John may have baptised by the mode of immersion; there does not appear to be evidence by which immersion could be disproved. Furthermore, if John baptised by the mode of immersion there is in this very consideration a good reason for choosing Jordan and Ainon as the sites of administration — there was abundant water in both places. And the expressions used with reference to Jordan, namely, "in the river Jordan" and "into the Jordan" could readily be taken as reflecting, to some extent at least, on the actual mode.[18] The point upon which emphasis must be placed is that the expressions used and the consideration mentioned in reference to Ainon, that there was much water there, do not prove that immersion was the mode and that the exigencies of immersion were the reasons

---

[18] *Cf.* John Gill: *op. cit.*, p. 308.

for choosing Jordan and Ainon. There are several other sufficient reasons why Jordan and Ainon should have been chosen. We know only too well that in Palestine water supplies were jealously prized and guarded, and we know how friction sometimes developed over the use of water supplies. To say the least, it would have been prejudicial to John's ministry for him to have baptised except where there was abundant water. Large multitudes came to John's baptism. It would have been disrupting to a local community and an interference with their needs for large multitudes to congregate around limited water supplies. Apart from the actual water used for baptism, it would have been interference amounting to impropriety to deprive people of ready access to the water supply requisite for their daily needs.

Again, apart from the consideration of the water used in baptism and apart from the impropriety of interference with the needs of a local community, it would be necessary to seek a place of much water in order to meet the needs of those who congregated. Oftentimes the people who came to John's baptism came long distances. In many cases it is altogether likely that animals were used for conveyance. Those who came would therefore need water for their own use and for the use of the animals they may have brought. It is obvious that a place of much water would be indispensable.

We have thus a whole series of considerations which coalesce to show that a place of much water was requisite apart from the question of immersion. Hence the choosing of Jordan and Ainon does not prove that these places were selected because they afforded the amount of water requisite for immersion.

The expressions, "in the river Jordan" and "into the Jordan" do not prove immersion. As far as the expression "in the river Jordan" is concerned it may be nothing more than a designation of location just as "baptising in Ainon" in John 3:23 designates location. Consequently, the expression "in the river Jordan" proves nothing respecting the mode of John's baptism. And as far as the expression "into Jordan" is concerned we found already that even such an expression as "going down into the water" does not necessarily imply immersion. Standing in the water or on the brink of the river would satisfy completely the idea expressed.

(d) *Acts 2:41;10:47; 16:33.* These passages have sometimes been adduced to disprove immersion. But they establish no such conclusion. There is nothing in the actual circumstances of these instances of baptism which makes immersion impossible. On the other hand, there is nothing to suggest, far less to require, immersion. Hence it is far better not to appeal to such passages in this debate. An argument is only weakened in its effectiveness when it is supported by irrelevant or inconclusive data.

Conclusion. On the basis of such considerations as these, derived from both Old and New Testaments, we are led to the conclusion that though the word βαπτίζω and its cognates can be used to denote an action performed by immersion yet they may also be used to denote an action that can be performed by a variety of modes. Consequently the word βαπτίζω itself cannot be pleaded as an argument for the necessity of immersion as the mode of baptism.

It is still possible, however, that other evidence could be presented to show that immersion belongs to the essence of the symbolism. We turn, therefore, to the other phase of the Baptist argument in support of the thesis that immersion is the only proper mode of baptism.

B. *The Burial and Resurrection of Christ*

The two passages upon which the greater part of this phase of the argument for immersion rests are Romans 6:2–6; Colossians 2:11, 12. In essence the argument is that, since baptism represents union with Christ in his death and resurrection, immersion in water and emergence from it provide an analogy which graphically portrays that which is represented and sealed by baptism. Romans 6:3, 4 would appear to indicate such symbolism: "Or are ye ignorant that as many as were baptised into Christ Jesus were baptised into his death? Therefore we have been buried with him by baptism into death, in order that as Christ was raised from the dead through the glory of the Father, even so we should walk in newness of life." But more careful analysis will show that there is no necessary allusion to the mode of baptism.

It is beyond dispute that the leading thought of the apostle
here is that of union with Christ in his death, burial, and
resurrection. And verses 5 and 6 are confirmatory. They
carry on the same thought in different terms: "For if we have
become planted together in the likeness of his death, we shall
be also in that of the resurrection: knowing this that our old
man has been crucified with him, in order that the body of sin
might be destroyed, to the end that we should no longer serve
sin".

Paul is here dealing with the antinomian argument and, in
order to rebut it, he sets forth the particular phases of union
with Christ that are peculiarly adapted to that purpose,
namely, union with Christ in his death, burial, and resurrection.
He does this to show that every one who is united to Christ is,
by virtue of the efficacy of Christ's death and the power of his
resurrection, freed from the dominion of sin, lives a new resurrection life, and therefore cannot make his Christian faith
and profession a plea for, or an inducement to, continuance
in sin. Baptism, by which the Christian profession is registered
and sealed, means baptism into union with Christ, and Paul
is here stressing what such union means, particularly in reference to the death and resurrection of Christ. Believers died
with Christ, they were planted together in the likeness of his
death, they were buried with him, they were crucified with
him, they were raised up with him and planted together in the
likeness of his resurrection.

It is very easy to focus attention upon one or two of the
terms which Paul here uses and make it appear that the indispensable mode of baptism is after the analogy of what we have
arbitrarily selected. It is very easy to point to the expression
"buried with him" in verse 4 and insist that only immersion
provides any analogy to burial. But such procedure fails to
take account of all that Paul says here. It should be noted
that Paul not only says "buried together" (συνετάφημεν)
but also "planted together" (σύμφυτοι) and "crucified together" (συνεσταυρώθη). These latter expressions indicate
the union with Christ which is symbolised and sealed by baptism just as surely as does "buried together". But it is only
too apparent that they do not bear any analogy to immersion.
Even if it should be conceded that the different shades of

meaning possible in the case of "planted together" (σύμφυτοι) leave room for some resemblance to immersion, yet no resemblance can obtain in the case of "crucified together". We are represented as having been hung on the cross together with Christ, and that phase of union with Christ is represented by our baptism into Christ not one whit less than our death in him and our burial with him, not one whit less than our being planted with him in the likeness of his death and our being raised with him in the power of his resurrection. When all of Paul's expressions are taken into account we see that burial with Christ can be appealed to as providing an index to the mode of baptism no more than can crucifixion with him. And since the latter does not indicate the *mode* of baptism there is no validity to the argument that burial does. The fact is that there are many aspects to our union with Christ. It is arbitrary to select one aspect and find in the language used to set it forth the essence of the mode of baptism. Such procedure is indefensible unless it can be carried through consistently. It cannot be carried through consistently here and therefore it is arbitrary and invalid. This passage as a whole points up the arbitrariness of such procedure by emphasising a phase of our union with Christ that bears no analogy whatsoever to that of immersion.

Confirmatory of this conclusion is Galatians 3:27. Here another implication of our union with Christ is argued by the apostle. The form of statement is closely similar to that of Romans 6:3. In Romans 6:3 Paul says: "As many as were baptised into Christ were baptised into his death", and in Galatians 3:27: "For as many as were baptised into Christ did put on Christ". It would be just as legitimate to insist that there is reference to the mode of baptism in Galatians 3:27 as in Romans 6:3. But in Galatians 3:27 the figure used by the apostle to set forth the import of baptism into Christ has no resemblance to immersion. It is the figure of putting on a garment. The plain inference is that Paul is not alluding to the mode of baptism at all. And neither may we suppose that he is in Romans 6:2–6. We should be faced with contradictory testimony as to the mode of baptism if we supposed that these passages allude to it.

In I Corinthians 12:13 we have the same effect. "For by

one Spirit have we all been baptised into one body." The figure here is the making up of one unified organism and is quite foreign to the notion of immersion.

The only sane conclusion is that in none of these cases is reference made to the mode of baptism.[19] The emphasis is plainly upon the meaning of baptism into Christ, that is to say, of union with him. Indeed, so paramount is the thought of union with Christ that the allusion to the rite of baptism need not be considered as overt. While it might not be proper to say that allusion to the rite of baptism is not at all present in the use of the word "baptise" in these passages, yet in such expressions as "baptised into Christ", "baptised into his death" (Rom. 6:3; Gal. 3:27), and "baptised into one body" (I Cor. 12:13), it is not the rite of baptism that is in the foreground but rather the idea of union with Christ. "Being baptised into" is a way of expressing "union with". To be "baptised into Moses" (I Cor. 10:2) is to be bound to Moses in the fellowship of that covenant of which Moses was the mediator. In a word, it is to be a disciple of Moses. Paul protests to the Corinthians that they were not baptised "into the name of Paul" (I Cor. 1:13): it would have meant that they had been baptised into the discipleship of Paul rather than into that of Jesus. To be "baptised into Christ" is to be

---

[19] James Bannerman does not sufficiently take into account the data provided by the passages concerned when, with reference to Romans 6:3–5, he says: "There are two things which seem plainly enough to be included in this remarkable statement. *In the first place*, the immersion in water of the persons of those who are baptized is set forth as their burial with Christ in His grave because of sin; and their being raised again out of the water is their resurrection with Christ in His rising again from the dead because of their justification ... And *in the second place*, their burial in water, when dying with Christ, was the washing away of the corruptness of the old man beneath the water; and their coming forth from the water in the image of His resurrection was their leaving behind them the old man with his sins, and emerging into newness of life. Their immersion beneath the water, and their emerging again, were the putting off the corruption of nature and rising again into holiness, or their sanctification" (*op. cit.*, pp. 47 f.). Many commentators have found in Romans 6:4 an allusion to immersion. But see for the contrary: Edward Beecher: *op. cit.*, pp. 86 ff.; Moses Stuart: *A Commentary on the Epistle to the Romans* (Andover, 1835), pp. 272 ff.; Charles Hodge: *Commentary on the Epistle to the Romans* (Philadelphia, 1864), p. 305; Robert Wilson: *op. cit.*, pp. 286 ff.

bound to him in the bonds of that union that makes us the beneficiaries of all the blessings of redemption and pledges us to his Lordship. The rite of baptism is the sign and seal of this union. But the language of the symbol and seal becomes so closely attached to that which the symbol represents that this language may be used to express that truth when the symbol itself has receded into the background of thought. Hence in these passages which have been considered it is not the rite of baptism that is in the foreground. Indeed, reference to the rite may have receded almost to the point of disappearance. It is union with Christ that claims the thought, and the language of baptism has been appropriated to give emphasis to that thought as well as to express the fulness and richness of the union involved.

General Conclusion. We have seen that the two pillars of the Baptist argument for the necessity of immersion, when examined in the light of the evidence provided by the Scriptures themselves, do not rest upon solid foundations. The usage in respect of βαπτίζω and its cognates does not show that these terms imply immersion.[20] There are very few instances where it can be shown that they refer to immersion, and there are many instances where it can be shown that they refer to actions performed by other modes than that of immersion. βαπτίζω, therefore, does not mean to immerse. The collateral Baptist argument drawn from similitude to the burial and resurrection of Christ has been shown to rest upon an arbitrary selection of one or two texts, and the invalidity of this selection is demonstrated by the very passage which appears to give strongest support to the contention. βαπτίζω, we must conclude, is one of those words which indicate a certain effect without itself expressing or prescribing the particular mode by which this effect is secured.

---

[20] Even Calvin falls into the mistake of saying that "the very word *baptize* . . . signifies to immerse" (*Inst.* IV, xv, 19), though he argues in the same context that it is of no importance whether a person be wholly immersed or whether water be only poured or sprinkled.

III

The Church

Baptism is an ordinance instituted by Christ and is the sign and seal of union with him. This is just saying that it is the sign and seal of membership in that body of which Christ is the Head. The body of which Christ is the Head is the church (*cf.* Eph. 5:23–30). Hence baptism is the sign and seal of membership in the church. What then is the church?

The Church as Invisible

As has just been indicated, the church is the body of Christ. If so, it is comprised of those who are sanctified and cleansed by the washing of water by the Word, the company of the regenerate, the communion of the saints, the congregation of the faithful, those called effectually into the fellowship of Christ. The church is therefore circumscribed by the facts of regeneration and faith, facts which in themselves are spiritual and invisible. For this reason no man or organisation of men is able infallibly to determine who are regenerate and who are not, who are true believers and who are not. No man or organisation of human composition, therefore, is able to define the precise limits of the church in any one place or generation. The Lord knows them that are His and He alone perfectly and infallibly. Again, when we think of the innumerable company of those who, in all past ages of this world's history, have been called effectually by God's grace and translated from the power of darkness into the fellowship of God, we see even more clearly how impossible it is for man to measure the proportions or limits of the people of God. And, finally, when we contemplate the whole body of God's elect in all ages on to the consummation of the world we see most clearly that only God can comprehend such a body of redeemed and sanctified persons. For these reasons, if for no others, we must recognise that there is an aspect of invisibility that attaches to the concept of the church.[21]

It is to be admitted that such an attribute is not expressly predicated of the church in Scripture. It must also be used with great care and with the requisite qualifications. We may not properly speak of two churches, one visible and the other invisible. What Scripture designates as "the church" is never regarded as something wholly invisible. But since a distinction must be drawn between that which is visible to and observable by men, on the one hand, and that which is fully and perfectly perceptible to God alone, on the other, there is an attribute of invisibility which must be recognised as belonging to the church. To be quite concrete, our Lord himself did distinguish between those who might be disciples of his and yet not truly disciples ($\dot{a}\lambda\eta\theta\hat{\omega}s$ $\mu\alpha\theta\eta\tau\alpha\acute{\iota}$, John 8:31) and between those who were in him by profession and external connection and yet not vitally and permanently (John 15). Our approach to this question of the church must take account of the fact that every one who has a place in the organisation which is visible and known to men is not by that mere token necessarily united to Christ by regeneration and faith. It is the distinction between that which is visible to men and what is known and viewed only perfectly by God that is guarded by saying that there is to the church an aspect of invisibility. We cannot think properly of the church unless we recognise that the church is constituted by a relation to Christ which

[21] In order to avoid the misconstructions and misconceptions frequently associated with the distinction between the church visible and invisible it is more proper to speak of the church as invisible and the church as visible or of the aspects of invisibility and visibility attaching to the church rather than of the visible church and the invisible church. The terms visible and invisible are aspects from which the church may be viewed. James Bannerman states this well: "When we speak of the Church invisible and the Church visible, we are not to be understood as if we referred in these designations to two separate and distinct Churches, but rather to the same Church under two different characters. We do not assert that Christ has founded two Churches on earth, but only one; and we affirm that that one Church is to be regarded under two distinct aspects" (op. cit., Vol. I, p. 29). But Bannerman does not appear to carry out this emphasis consistently in his subsequent discussion. He proceeds to define the visible church and the invisible respectively in terms of distinctions which do not appear to be borne out by the usage of Scripture itself.

in itself is spiritual and invisible and that nothing observable
by men can be the absolute and final criterion of that relation.
The Lord knows them that are His.[22]

The Church as Visible

While the church in its strict and proper signification is the
company or body of those united to Christ in the spiritual
bonds of effectual calling and saving faith and is therefore
known only to God who alone infallibly discerns as well as
determines who His people are, yet it must not be thought
that the church, as Scripture knows it, is ever an invisible
entity. The church may not be defined as an entity wholly
invisible to human perception and observation. The church
is the company or society or assembly or congregation or
communion of the faithful. This concept has a variety of
applications. It may refer to a company or congregation of
believers in one house (*cf*. Rom. 16:5; I Cor. 16:19; Col. 4:15;
Phm. 2). It may refer to the company of believers in one city
(*cf*. Acts 8:1; 11:22, 26; 13:1; 14:27; 15:22; 18:22; 20:17; Rom.
16:1).[23] It may refer to the company of believers in a
province (*cf*. Acts 9:31). Very frequently the word is used in
the plural to designate the plurality of churches, that is to
say of units, scattered throughout a certain area of lesser or
greater geographical proportions (*cf*. Acts 14:23; 15:41; I Cor.
16:1, 19; II Cor. 8:1; Gal. 1:2, 22; I. Thess. 2:14), or scattered
throughout the whole world (*cf*. Rom. 16:4, 16; I Cor. 7:17;
11:16; 14:33, 34; II Cor. 8:18; 11:28; II Thess. 1:4). Sometimes it is used in the singular, not in the sense of a particular
company of believers in one place, but in a generic sense to
designate the people of God in their unity and totality (I Cor.
10:32; 12:28; 15:9; Gal. 1:13; Eph. 1:22; 3:10, 21; 5:23, 24, 25,
27, 29, 32; Col. 1:18, 24). This last feature of New Testament
usage provides us with the concept of the church catholic or

---

[22] *Cf*. Calvin: *Inst*. IV, i, 2.

[23] *Cf*. James Bannerman: *op. cit*., Vol. I, pp. 13 f. for a treatment of
the data which show that the *church* in Jerusalem, for example, did not
apply "to a single congregation of believers, but to a plurality of congre-
gations, connected together as one body or Church by means of a common
government".

universal. A thorough study of this usage would evince that
there are several aspects from which the church catholic, or
the church considered generically, may be viewed. It would
be going too far afield to undertake such a study now. But
a brief examination of the passages cited above from Paul's
epistles to the Ephesians and to the Colossians will show
how expansive and inclusive the word "church" is in such
connections.

What needs to be particularly observed in connection with
the New Testament is that whether the church is viewed as
the unit or company of believers in a home or town or city,
or whether it is viewed as the broader communion of the
saints scattered throughout a province, or the whole company
of believers scattered throughout the world, it is always a
visible observable entity. Union with Christ and the faith
through which that union is effected, though in themselves
invisible and spiritual facts, are nevertheless realities which
find expression in what is observable. Faith always receives
registration in word and action. This is just saying that those
united to Christ form the communion of the saints and the
congregation of the faithful. And what is even more relevant
and important is that by the appointment and prescription
of Christ as the Head of the church there is the institution
which by its very nature as an institution of Christ in the
world is a visible and observable entity. The people of God
do come together and associate with one another for purposes
of collective testimony and worship, for the administration of
divinely instituted ordinances, for mutual edification, and
for the exercise of divinely instituted government and discipline. The very constitutive idea of the church, namely, union
with Christ and the union of believers with one another in the
body of Christ, as an idea realised in the history of this world,
necessarily involves visible union and communion. We cannot
think of the church invisible as anything that exists in abstraction or apart from the overt expression which the spiritual and invisible facts of union and communion with Christ
demand. Hence visible association and organisation are implicit in the very nature of what constitutes the church. Such
organisation is effected by the efficacious and continuous work-
ing of the Head of the church through his Word and Spirit,

and human agency and responsibility which are exercised in pursuance of Christ's institution bear the seal of his authorisation and command. All of this is implied in our Lord's word, "Upon this rock I will build my church; and the gates of hell shall not prevail against it" (Matt. 16:18). In a word, the church is Christ's church. It is established and preserved by him, and its continuance as an entity to be administered in accordance with his institution is guaranteed by the fact that he is Head over all things to his body the church.

As was indicated above, human agency and responsibility are operative in the church. One of the ways in which this agency is exercised is the administration which is committed to men. There is government and discipline in Christ's church and such are administered by men, in accordance with Christ's appointment. The question arises at this point: how does this administration on the part of men relate itself to those spiritual and invisible facts by which the church is constituted? Men are not omniscient, and they, are fallible. What is the prerogative of fallible men in reference to this all-important phase of the administration exercised by them, namely, the inclusion of members in, and exclusion from, the visible church? In other words, what are the criteria by which men are to judge in the exercise of this responsibility which is committed to them? The church is not a haphazard assemblage or organisation. It is the communion of the saints and has specific character determined by the specific character of those constituting it and by the specific purposes for which they are associated together. It is not a voluntary society in the sense that the members and officers may by their own prerogative or discretion devise the terms and conditions of association. These terms are prescribed by the Head of the church: the church is the institute of Christ.

What we find in the New Testament is that the constituting bond of communion was common faith in Christ and that the condition of admission to the fellowship was this same common faith (cf. Acts 2:38–42; 8:13, 35–38; 10:34–38; 16:14, 15, 31–33). This faith, however, did not have any automatic way of evidencing itself and, consequently, could become effective in gaining admission to the fellowship of the saints only by confession or profession. This means that faith was registered by confession, and the criterion by which the church exercised its administrative responsibility in the admission of members was confession. In its essence this confession was that Jesus was the Christ, the Son of God, and that he was Lord. Such a confession had far-reaching implications for faith and conduct even within the sphere of human judgment. Mere lip confession, contradicted by other evidence either in the realm of faith or conduct, could not be accepted for entrance into or continuance in the fellowship of the saints. We may, therefore, define the confession as an intelligent and consistent profession of faith in Christ and of obedience to him. It is obvious that such confession falls within the orbit in which human discrimination and judgment may be exercised. It is not the prerogative of man to search the heart of another. But it is the prerogative of man to judge in reference to public confession or profession. This, therefore, is the criterion in accord with which human administration is exercised. And what needs to be emphasised here is that this is so by divine institution. It is not the expedient of proven experience. And it is not simply a necessity arising from the limitations inherent in human nature. It is by divine institution that the church, as a visible entity administered by men in accordance with Christ's appointment, must admit to its fellowship those who make a credible profession of faith in Christ and promise of obedience to him. To exclude such is to arrogate to ourselves prerogatives which do not belong to us and it is to violate the institution of Christ.

This profession, though it is a profession that only a true believer can honestly and truly make, is, nevertheless, of such a nature that those who do not have true faith may make it to the satisfaction of those responsible for that administration whereby admission is secured into the fellowship of the church (*cf.* Acts 8:13, 20–23). We are here faced with the anomaly that the visible entity which is called the church may comprise within its membership those who do not really and truly belong to the body of Christ. Even when human vigilance is exercised to the fullest extent of its prerogative, people may be admitted to the church, and necessarily admitted as far as human administration is concerned, who do not really belong to the church of Christ. This is an anomaly which

must be fully appreciated and we must not make attempts to
eliminate it. There are two dangers we must avoid and into
which we are too liable to fall.[24]

The first danger is to construe the confession as not a confession of true and saving faith but simply of intellectual and
historical faith.[25] In this way it might appear that the dis-

[24] For a history of thought and debate on this question in New England
in the seventeenth and eighteenth centuries, centering particularly around
what has been called the Half-Way Covenant, cf. Williston Walker: *The
Creeds and Platforms of Congregationalism*, Chapter XI, (New York, 1893),
pp. 238–339.

[25] The position developed in the pages which follow is that of the
Reformed Churches in their representative and classic expressions. It is
set forth, for example, in the Westminster Standards. The Westminster
Confession says: "Sacraments are holy signs and seals of the covenant of
grace, immediately instituted by God, to represent Christ, and His benefits,
and to confirm our interest in Him: as also, to put a visible difference
between those that belong unto the Church, and the rest of the world; and
solemnly to engage them to the service of God in Christ, according to His
Word" (Chapter XXVII, Section I). And the Larger Catechism even
more explicitly says: "A sacrament is an holy ordinance instituted by
Christ in his church, to signify, seal, and exhibit unto those that are within
the covenant of grace, the benefits of his mediation; to strengthen and
increase their faith, and all other graces; to oblige them to obedience; to
testify and cherish their love and communion one with another; and to
distinguish them from those that are without" (Question 162). With reference to baptism the Confession says: "Baptism is a sacrament of the
new testament, ordained by Jesus Christ, not only for the solemn admission
of the party baptized into the visible Church; but also, to be unto him a
sign and seal of the covenant of grace, of his ingrafting into Christ, of
regeneration, of remission of sins, and of his giving up unto God, through
Jesus Christ, to walk in newness of life" (Chapter XXVIII, Section I).
And the Larger Catechism: "Baptism is a sacrament of the New Testament,
wherein Christ hath ordained the washing with water in the name of the
Father, and of the Son, and of the Holy Ghost, to be a sign and seal of
ingrafting into himself, of remission of sins by his blood, and regeneration
by his Spirit; of adoption, and resurrection unto everlasting life; and
whereby the parties baptized are solemnly admitted into the visible
church, and enter into open and professed engagement to be wholly and
only the Lord's" (Question 165). *Cf.* the Shorter Catechism, Questions 92
and 94.

William Cunningham with his usual thoroughness and erudition has
dealt with this question and has set forth the classic Reformed position in
distinction from the Lutheran position and also in distinction from de-
formations and aberrations that have crept into Churches professing the
Reformed confession (see the essay, "Zwingle and the Doctrine of the

crepancy between the fact that the church consists of those
who are members of the body of Christ and the fact that many
may be admitted into the fellowship of the visible church who
are not truly members of the body of Christ is removed. It is
a false solution. There is no warrant whatsoever for supposing
that the confession which we find in the New Testament, by
which members were admitted into the fellowship of the
church, was a profession of mere intellectual or historical
belief. It was the confession of like nature with that which
Peter made at Caesarea Philippi, a confession which elicited
from our Lord the benediction, "Blessed art thou, Simon
Bar-jona: for flesh and blood hath not revealed it unto thee,
but my Father which is in heaven" (Matt. 16:17). It is most
instructive in this regard that the confession of Peter provided
the occasion for the most significant disclosure made by our
Lord respecting the church: "Upon this rock I will build my
church" (Matt. 16:18). However we may interpret the word
"rock" in this utterance there can be no question but that
the church confession is the kind of confession made by Peter.
And this means that the confession requisite for membership
in the church is the confession of Jesus as the Christ, as the
Son of God, as Saviour, and as Lord. It is a profession of
true and saving faith.

It is not by any means the prerogative of those who administer the government and discipline of the church to determine
whether the profession made is a true and sincere profession
of such faith. A judgment of this kind would exceed the
warrant of men. But it is the prerogative and duty of those
who rule in the church of God to make plain, both in the instruction and examination of candidates for admission, what
the meaning of the profession is and to insist that only the
regenerate, only those united to Christ by faith, can truly
make the profession required. There is thus the fullest scope

Sacraments" in *The Reformers and the Theology of the Reformation*, 1866,
pp. 262–291). Of particular interest is the quotation from Martin Vitringa
in which we have a summary of the doctrine of the Reformed Churches
on this point (*ibid.*, pp. 264 f.). The quotations also from Samuel Ruther-
ford, George Gillespie, Thomas Boston, and John Erskine are most pertinent and instructive. See also Charles Hodge: *Systematic Theology* (New
York, 1873), Vol. III, pp. 562 ff.

for the examination of candidates in ascertaining the intelligence and consistency of the profession made, in instructing
candidates respecting the nature of the Christian confession,
in dissuading those who do not have true faith from making
the profession which they cannot sincerely and honestly make,
and in maintaining the purity of the church against the entrance of the ignorant and profane. But this examination, it
must be remembered, is not conducted on the premise that
to the officers of the church or to the church as a communion
is given the prerogative to determine who are regenerate and
who are not. It is conducted, rather, on the basis that to the
ministry of the church belongs the obligation to insure as far
as possible by instruction and warning that only those united
to Christ will make the confession which only such can truly
make. It is the function of the church to demand an intelligent, credible, and uncontradicted confession that Jesus is
the Christ, the Son of the living God.

The second danger that must be avoided is the tendency
to define the church in such a way as would seem to eliminate
or at least tone down the discrepancy or anomaly with which
we are dealing. This again is a mistake. Our definition of the
church must not be framed in terms of an accommodation by
which we make provision, *within our definition*, for the inclusion of hypocrites, that is to say, of those who profess to be
Christ's but are not really his. Our definition of the church
must be framed in terms of the constitutive principle, to wit,
that the church consists of those who are united to Christ and
are members of his body. It is the communion of saints. And
it is precisely that body of believers in fellowship with Christ
and with one another, associated together in the world in
accordance with Christ's institution, which is called in the
New Testament "the church" and is what we often call the
visible church. We may not abandon this constitutive principle, we may not accommodate our definition in order to make
allowance for the fact that some make the profession who do
not have the faith and who enter into the fellowship without
the bond that constitutes it.[26]

[26] It is very easy to fall into this kind of accommodation when we begin
to apply the distinction between the church as invisible and the church as
visible. And, indeed, it may appear to be necessary in order to avoid other

Perhaps no passage evinces this more clearly than Paul's salutation to the church at Corinth in his first epistle: "Paul called to be an apostle of Christ Jesus through the will of God, and Sosthenes our brother, to the church of God which is at Corinth, to them who are sanctified in Christ Jesus, called to be saints, with all those who call upon the name of our Lord Jesus Christ, their Lord and ours" (I Cor. 1:1, 2). However we may construe the precise syntactic relation which the expression, "the church of God which is at Corinth", sustains to the two clauses which immediately follow, it would be exegetical violence to think that the church of God at Corinth may be construed in other terms than the "sanctified in Christ Jesus" and the "called to be saints", as also those at Corinth who "call upon the name of our Lord Jesus Christ". In other words, this provides us with Paul's concept of the church at Corinth, namely, those sanctified in Christ Jesus and called to be saints, and he does not conceive of the church in broader terms so as to distinguish between the church and those sanctified and called. In this epistle this is all the more illumining because in chapter 5 he proceeds to deal with those who had made the Christian profession and who were in the fellowship of the church but who by reason of gross sin were to be excluded from its communion. In dealing with the incestuous person he demands the delivering of "such a person unto Satan for the destruction of the flesh" and adds, "Know ye not that a little leaven leavens the whole lump? Purge out therefore the old leaven, that ye may be a new lump, as ye are unleavened" (vss. 6, 7). He continues the subject of discipline and says, "If any one that is called a brother be a fornicator, or covetous, or an idolater, or a railer, or a drunk-

pitfalls, especially the pitfall of the Romish doctrine of the church. In the esteem of the present writer this appears rather conspicuously in James Bannerman's excellent work, *The Church of Christ*. His definition of the visible church is framed in terms that do not appear to be supported by New Testament usage (*cf. op. cit.*, Vol. I, pp. 29 ff.). The terms in which Bannerman develops the distinction between visible and invisible and frames his definition of the visible church seem to provide us with a very simple and effective polemic against Rome. The controversy with Rome must, of course, be unabated, but it does not appear to be sound to conduct this controversy on the basis of a definition which does not find its counterpart in the Biblical usage with reference to the church.

ard, or a thief; with such an one no not to eat" (vs. 11). Paul recognises that people bearing the Christian name and therefore
admitted to the fellowship of the church might be proven to
be or turn out to be profane persons having no inheritance in
the kingdom of God (*cf.* 6:9, 10). He commands that such
be put outside the fellowship of the church (*cf.* 5:13). He
recognised the facts which arose from the sinfulness and in-
firmity of fallen human nature. But the instructive feature
of this epistle is that when Paul addressed the church and
conceived of it he did not construe the church at Corinth in
such terms as would allow for the inclusion, in what he defines
as the church, of those persons who might have borne the
Christian name and been admitted to the communion of the
saints but who were not sanctified in Christ Jesus and called
to be saints. Paul recognised that there was old leaven in the
church at Corinth, leaven which needed to be purged out.
But when he addresses the church he does not address it as
a community to be defined in terms of old leaven and new
unleavened bread. He does not define the church in terms
which would make allowance for both elements. No, he addresses the church as those sanctified in Christ Jesus, called
to be saints, and who call upon the name of the Lord Jesus
Christ. Other salutations of Paul are to the same effect.
I Thessalonians 1:1 and II Thessalonians 1:1 are particularly
relevant. He salutes the church at Thessalonica as "the church
of the Thessalonians in God the Father and the Lord Jesus
Christ" (I Thess. 1:1; *cf.* Rom. 1:7; II Cor. 1:1; Eph. 1:1;
Phil. 1:1; Col. 1:2).

It is true that hypocrites may secure admission to the
church. As we have seen, the very administration which
Christ has instituted for the admission of members allows for
that. There are disciples who are not truly disciples, and there
are branches in the vine which are not vitally and abidingly
in the vine. But while we fully recognise this fact we must at
the same time distinguish between the constitutive principle
in terms of which the church is defined, on the one hand, and
the *de facto* situation arising from the way in which Christ
has chosen to administer the affairs of his church in the world,
on the other. The inclusion and exclusion are in the hands
of fallible men. This administration is of divine institution.

Hence those who are not Christ's gain admission.[27] Here is
the anomaly. We have to recognise and contain it. It persists in its sharpness because we refuse to define the church in
lower terms than the body of Christ and the communion of the
saints. It is that definition that creates the anomaly and we
may not revise the definition in order to relieve the tension.
For the anomaly in this case is just one way in which the discrepancy between God's secret and infallible operations, on
the one hand, and the way by which He has pleased to administer the means of grace in the world, on the other, appears.
This discrepancy manifests itself in other connections. And
we must not attempt to remove the discrepancy by eliminating
or modifying the truths which create it. In this case it means
that we must continue to define the church as the body of
Christ, the *congregatio fidelium*, the *communio sanctorum*.

Baptism is the sign and seal of membership in the church. It
is administered, therefore, to those who make the requisite
confession of faith in Jesus. According to our Lord's institution in the great commission baptism in the name of the Father
and of the Son and of the Holy Ghost is an integral part of
the process of discipling the nations and is therefore an essential mark of discipleship. Baptism is not an addendum to
discipleship but that by which discipleship is consummated.
And discipleship comes to fruition and receives its vindication
in the observance of all things which Jesus has commanded.
In the terms of the great commission the church consists of
those who are disciples. Since discipleship is not consummated
without baptism we must regard baptism as an indispensable
mark of the church. The person who refuses baptism and
declines the reproach of Christ, which it entails, cannot be
received as a member of Christ's body. And the organisation

[27] *Cf.* Calvin: *Inst.* IV, i, 7 and 8.

In refraining from the attempt to define the church in terms of an accommodation that will make allowance for the inclusion of hypocrites we are
following the same lines as would have to be followed in defining the kingdom of God. We are not forgetful of the parables of the tares and the wheat
and of the drag net. There is a mixture in the kingdom, and Christ will at
the end gather out of his kingdom all things that offend and them which
do iniquity. But we may not *define* the kingdom of God in terms of accommodation to this *de facto* situation. We must define it in terms of the rule
and realm of righteousness, life, and peace.

which discards baptism and thereby evinces its rejection of the authority and Lordship of Christ cannot be accounted a branch of the Christian church.

The Church Generically One

It is necessary to distinguish between the form of the visible church under the Old Testament and its form under the New. Such a distinction is implied in the words of our Lord to Peter: "Thou art Peter, and upon this rock I will build my church; and the gates of hell shall not prevail against it" (Matt. 16:18). Jesus was referring to the new form which the church was to assume in consequence of his own messianic work. He calls it "my church". Full allowance must be made for the new form of structure and administration established by the death, resurrection, and ascension of Christ and the outpouring of the Holy Spirit at Pentecost. Nevertheless the distinction does not warrant the denial of the existence of the church under the Old Testament, nor of the generic unity and continuity of the church in both dispensations. In addition to the fact that the organisation of the people of God in the Old Testament is expressly called the church (Acts 7:38), we must bear in mind that the church in the New Testament is founded upon the covenant made with Abraham. The specific covenant administration under which the New Testament church operates is the extension and unfolding of the Abrahamic covenant. This is distinctly the argument of the apostle Paul in the epistle to the Galatians when he says, "they which be of faith are blessed with faithful Abraham" and that the "covenant, confirmed beforehand by God, the law which was four hundred and thirty years afterward does not make void, so as to make the promise of no effect" (Gal. 3:9, 17). It is the blessing of Abraham, a blessing secured to him by the covenant administered to him, that comes upon the Gentiles through Christ (Gal. 3:14). The church as it exists in the respective dispensations is not two organisms. It is likened to one tree with many branches, all of which grow from one root and stock and form one organic life (Rom. 11:16–21). Paul again reminds us that while the Gentiles were at one time "aliens from the commonwealth of Israel and strangers from the covenants

of promise", yet now in Christ Jesus they are "no more
strangers and foreigneis, but fellow-citizens with the saints
and of the household of God, being built upon the foundation
of the apostles and prophets, Christ Jesus himself being the
chief corner stone" (Eph. 2:12, 19, 20). There is generic
unity, continuity, and identity. Only within this generic unity
may the specific distinctions be recognised and applied. It is
putting the matter mildly when we say that there are principles, common to both dispensations, which are operative in,
and must be recognised as applying to, the distinct forms
which the church assumed in the respective dispensations.
Perhaps no other datum is more relevant and conclusive to
establish the unity and continuity of the church in both econ-
omies than the fact that the New Testament is the expansion
and unfolding of the Abrahamic covenant, that all nations
are blessed in terms of the promise given to Abraham, "In
thee shall all the families of the earth be blessed" (Gen. 12:3),
that Abraham is the father of the faithful, and that New
Testament believers of all nations are Abraham's seed and
heirs according to promise. It is this basic and underlying
unity of the covenant of grace and of promise that establishes
the generic unity and continuity of the church. In terms of
covenant union and communion the church is but the covenant
people of God in all ages and among all nations. The promise
which epitomises the unity, and which summarises the constitutive principle, of the church is, "I will be their God, and
they shall be my people". This is the promise of grace upon
which rests the communion of the people of God in all ages.
It applies to the New Testament as well as to the Old and to
the Old no less than to the New. It is also the bond that unites
them inseparably together.

IV

Infant Baptism

If it is proper to administer baptism to infants, then the import of baptism must be the same for infants as for adults. It cannot have one meaning for infants and another for adults. Baptism is the sign and seal of membership in Christ's body, the church. If the baptism of infants is of divine institution, baptism must be for them, no less than for adults, the sign and seal of union with Christ in the virtue of his death and the power of his resurrection. As we proceed to set forth the argument in support of infant baptism it is necessary to bear in mind all that has been said already respecting the nature of the church, particularly the tenet that the church is generically one in both dispensations. The basic premise of the argument for infant baptism is that the New Testament economy is the unfolding and fulfilment of the covenant made with Abraham and that the necessary implication is the unity and continuity of the church.

The Inclusion of Infants

It is a fact beyond dispute that the covenant made with Abraham included the infant offspring of Abraham. This is just saying that the church under the Old Testament included not only all who were of sufficient age and intelligence to confess the true religion but also their infant seed. Infants received the sign of circumcision. It was administered to them by divine command (Gen. 17:10–12). And circumcision was the sign and seal of the covenant administered to Abraham.

With reference to circumcision it must be fully appreciated that it was not essentially or primarily the sign of family, racial, or national identity. Any significance which circum-

cision possessed along the line of national identity or privilege
was secondary and derived. Its primary and essential significance was that it was the sign and seal of the highest and
richest spiritual blessing which God bestows upon men. This
is apparent from the following considerations.

1. In Genesis 17:1–14 we have what is probably the
fullest account of the covenant made with Abraham. It is,
in any case, basic and it clearly establishes the most relevant
principles. The covenant made with Abraham is that in
terms of which he received the promise that in him all the
families of the earth would be blessed. It is in terms of this
covenant that he is the father of all the faithful. It is this
covenant that is unfolded in the New Testament and it is
in terms of this covenant that the blessing of Abraham comes
upon the Gentiles. That circumcision is the sign of this covenant in the highest reaches of its meaning and in its deepest
spiritual significance is demonstrated by the fact that circumcision is called the covenant. "This is my covenant which ye
shall keep, between me and you, and thy seed after thee:
every male among you shall be circumcised" (vs. 10). "And
my covenant shall be in your flesh for an everlasting covenant" (vs. 13). "And the uncircumcised male who is not
circumcised . . . shall be cut off from among his people: he
hath broken my covenant" (vs. 14). Stephen reflects the
proper perception of this association when he says, "And he
gave him the covenant of circumcision" (Acts 7:8). This
mode of statement in Genesis 17 and in Stephen's speech
demonstrates that circumcision was the seal of the covenant
in its deepest spiritual significance. And we have no authority
whatsoever to say that circumcision was simply the sign of
an external relationship or of merely racial and national identity. It is indeed true that the spiritual blessing of the covenant made with Abraham carried with it external privileges
and it marked off the chosen people as a distinct national
and racial entity (*cf.* Gen. 12:2; 46:3; Deut. 4:7, 8, 34; I Chron.
17:21, 22). But these external blessings and national privileges accrued from the spiritual blessing which the covenant
embodied and imparted. In like manner circumcision, as the
sign and seal of the covenant, carried with it these external

blessings and national privileges. It was inevitable that cir-cumcision should have been associated with these national advantages that were derived from the blessing involved in and conveyed by the covenant. But it is a grave mistake to think of circumcision as the sign and seal of merely external blessings and privileges. Circumcision is the sign and seal of the covenant itself in its deepest and richest significance, and it is the sign of external privileges only as these are the fruits of the spiritual blessing which it signifies. It is then the sign of external blessing no more than is the covenant a covenant of external blessing. The covenant embraces external bles-sing but it does so only insofar as the internal blessing results in external manifestation. The covenant itself may not be identified with such manifestations. Neither may circumcision.

What was the Abrahamic covenant in the highest reaches of its meaning? Undeniably and simply: "I will be your God, and ye shall be my people" (cf. Gen. 17:7; Exod. 19:5, 6; Deut. 7:6; 14:2; Jer. 31:33). In a word it is union and com-munion with Jehovah, the God of Israel. It was this blessing circumcision signified and sealed.

2. The foregoing conclusions drawn from the study of Genesis 17:1–14 may also be elicited from the meaning at-tached to circumcision in other passages and contexts. Such passages as Exodus 6:12, 30; Leviticus 19:23; 26:41; Deuter-onomy 10:16; 30:6; Jeremiah 4:4; 6:10; 9:25 will show that circumcision carries the import of the removal of defilement. It means therefore the removal of that defilement with which even infants are afflicted and with which they enter this world. As symbolic of such defilement and its removal we readily see how it could have become the fitting sign of the covenant that secured union and communion with Jehovah. It signified and sealed that cleansing which fitted for the presence of Jehovah and so was the seal of union and communion.

3. Paul distinctly says that circumcision was the seal of the righteousness of the faith Abraham had while he was uncircumcised (Rom. 4:11; Col. 2:11, 12; Rom. 2:25–29; Phil. 3:3). It is therefore the seal of the righteousness of faith. And this is just saying that it is the seal of justification by

faith. How closely related this is to the more comprehensive notion of union and communion with God need not be argued.

These three notions — union and communion with God, the removal of defilement, and the righteousness of faith — are, obviously, not antithetical. They are mutually complementary, and, taken together, they indicate the deep soteric richness of the blessing that circumcision signifies and seals. It is no peripheral or external blessing that circumcision portrays any more than is it a peripheral blessing that the covenant imparts.

We cannot but recognise the close similarity that there is between these three elements of the import of circumcision and the three elements of the import of baptism which we discovered earlier in our discussion. Of particular note is the fact that the leading notion in the meaning of circumcision is identical in principle with the leading notion in the meaning of baptism, namely, union and communion with the Lord. And it is of paramount importance to take due account of the fact that it was by divine institution and command that the sign and seal of such blessing was administered to infants in the old economy. Circumcision, signifying what in principle is identical with that signified by baptism, was administered to infants who were born within the covenant relation and privilege.

The Continuance of this Privilege

The gospel dispensation is the unfolding of the covenant made with Abraham, the extension and enlargement of the blessing conveyed by this covenant to the people of the Old Testament period. Abraham is the father of all the faithful. They who are of faith are blessed with faithful Abraham. We come now to the question which cannot be suppressed or evaded and which cannot be pressed with too much emphasis. If children born of the faithful were given the sign and seal of the covenant and therefore of the richest blessing which the covenant disclosed, if the New Testament economy is the elaboration and extension of this covenant of which circumcision was the sign, are we to believe that infants in this age are excluded from that which was provided by the Abrahamic covenant? In other words, are we to believe that infants now may not properly be given the sign of that blessing which is enshrined in the new covenant? Is the new covenant in this respect less generous than was the Abrahamic? Is there less efficacy, as far as infants are concerned, in the new covenant than there was in the old?[28] Are infants in the new dispensation more *inhabile* to the grace of God? These are questions that cannot be lightly dismissed. And they are particularly pertinent and cogent when we remember that baptism, which is the sign of the covenant under the new economy as circumcision was under the old, bears essentially the same import as did circumcision. Baptism does not signify any higher kind of divine blessing than did circumcision. It may indicate more fully what the blessing is and how it is to be attained. But it does not signify any greater blessing. Shall we then say that baptism may not be administered to infants?

If infants are excluded now, it cannot be too strongly emphasised that this change implies a complete reversal of the earlier divinely instituted practice. So we must ask: do we find any hint or intimation of such reversal in either the Old or the New Testament? More pointedly, does the New Testament revoke or does it provide any intimation of revoking so expressly authorised a principle as that of the inclusion of infants in the covenant and their participation in the covenant sign and seal? This practice had been followed, by divine authority, in the administration of the covenant of grace for some two thousand years. Has it been discontinued? Our answer to these questions must be that we find

---

[28] Again the statement of Calvin is worth quoting: "The covenant is common, the reason for confirming it is common. Only the mode of confirmation is different; for to them it was confirmed by circumcision, which among us is succeeded by baptism. Otherwise, if the testimony by which the Jews were confirmed concerning the salvation of their seed be taken away from us, by the advent of Christ it has come to pass that the grace of God is more obscure and less attested to us than it was to the Jews. If this cannot be affirmed without the greatest dishonour to Christ ... we must confess that at least it ought not to be more concealed nor less attested than under the obscure shadows of the law" (*Inst.* IV, xvi, 6).

no evidence of revocation. In view of the fact that the new covenant is based upon and is the unfolding of the Abrahamic covenant, in view of the basic identity of meaning attaching to circumcision and baptism, in view of the unity and continuity of the covenant grace administered in both dispensations, we can affirm with confidence that evidence of revocation or repeal is mandatory if the practice or principle has been discontinued under the New Testament.

In the absence of such evidence of repeal we conclude that the administering of the sign and seal of the covenant to the infant seed of believers is still in operation and has perpetual divine warrant.[29] In other words, the command to administer the sign to infants has not been revoked: therefore it is still in force. The situation is that instead of requiring an express statute authorising the administration of baptism to infants we find, rather, that an express statute of this nature would be superfluous and therefore not necessary to the propriety and authority of this ordinance.

Again, the case is not simply that we possess no evidence of repeal of this divinely instituted practice in the administration of God's grace in the world. In addition we have some positive evidence in favour of its continuance, not in the form of an express statute, for in that case there would be no dispute, but in the form of data which cannot be properly assessed unless we regard the principle which underlies circumcision as still valid and in operation under the New Testament. With that evidence we shall deal later.

Finally, we cannot believe that the New Testament economy is less beneficent than was the Old. It is rather the case that the New Testament gives more abundant scope to the blessing of God's covenant. We are not therefore led to expect retraction; we are led to expect expansion and extension. It would not accord with the genius of the new economy to suppose that there is the abrogation of so cardinal a method of disclosing and applying the grace which lies at the heart of God's covenant administration.

[29] Cf. John Lightfoot: Works (ed. Pitman), London, 1823, Vol. XI, p. 58; Richard Baxter: Plain Scripture Proof of Infants Church-membership and Baptism, London, 1653, pp. 38 ff.; Robert Wilson: op. cit., pp. 438 ff.

The Significance of Infant Baptism

Though circumcision and baptism are the signs and seals of covenant union and communion, it does not follow that every one who bears this sign and seal is an actual partaker of the grace signified and sealed and is therefore an heir of eternal life. It frequently happens that the sign is administered to those who, from the standpoint of good government and discipline, ought not to be baptised. The church too often fails to maintain the proper oversight and discrimination in this matter as in all others. But apart from the question of looseness and carelessness in administering this rite, it does not even follow that all those who, from the viewpoint of administration, properly bear the sign and seal are possessors of the actual grace signified. That is to say, even when the church exercises the proper oversight and discipline, even when all the safeguards of divine institution are applied, it does not follow that the administration of this rite insures for the recipient the possession of the grace signified. It must be admitted that this appears very anomalous, and it presents us with great difficulty. There have been many attempts made to resolve the difficulty.

It should be remembered that this anomaly does not concern infant baptism alone: it is a difficulty that inheres in the question of the baptism of adults as well. Antipaedobaptists must not think that they enjoy any immunity from this question, although they may sometimes naively consider that it is the exclusive problem of paedobaptists. It is a question that concerns the import of the sacraments as such. Here, however, we are concerned with this general question as it applies to infant baptism. And it is conceded that the question arises for many people most acutely in connection with the baptism of infants.

Several observations call for very distinct emphasis in connection with this question.

1. We must not seek the solution of the anomaly by saying that circumcision and baptism are signs and seals merely of *external* covenant privilege and blessing, that is to say, of external relationship as distinguished from the internal and spiritual blessing dispensed in and through the covenant of

grace. It cannot be too insistently stressed that circumcision was and baptism is the sign and seal of the covenant in the highest reaches and deepest significance of its soteric and spiritual meaning. In a word, they are signs and seals of the covenant of grace, not of certain external blessings accruing from or following upon the covenant of grace. And this is so even though many who bear the sign and seal do not possess and may never possess the blessings of the covenant itself.

It is not being contended that the distinction between an external covenant relationship and the internal covenant relationship is necessarily improper. This indeed may be a proper and even necessary distinction. Neither is it contended that it is improper to say that there have been and are many who have enjoyed the privileges of the external covenant relationship who are not partakers of the blessing of the covenant of grace. What is being contended for is that baptism may never properly be said to be the sign and seal of the external relationship rather than of the covenant itself in its richest and deepest blessing. There is not the slightest warrant from Scripture for the notion that baptism or, for that matter, circumcision is simply the sign and seal of external privilege.

2. The resolution of the anomaly, that there are some who, from the standpoint of administration, rightly receive the sign and seal of that which in reality they do not possess, is not to be sought along the line of the distinction between an external covenant relationship and the internal spiritual relationship but rather in the consideration that there is a discrepancy between the secret operations and purposes of God in his saving grace, on the one hand, and the divinely instituted method of administering the covenant in the world, on the other. In other words, the administration of the rite that is the sign and seal of the covenant has to be conducted not in accordance with God's secret operations and infallible purposes of grace but in accordance with certain requirements which fallible men may execute and apply. The divine method of administering the covenant in the world is that God commits to fallible men the ordinances of administration. These ordinances have to be dispensed in accordance with require-

ments which fallible men may apply. But the requirements
that may be applied by men are not the measure of God's
secret and efficacious operations of grace. To be very specific,
baptism is not administered by revelation of God's secret
will. It is properly administered when certain conditions of
divine prescription, conditions with reference to which fallible
men are in a position to judge, have been fulfilled. This is
the divine institution. But God has not given us any assurance that the operations of His saving grace are invariably
present where the divine institution is observed. Consequently, among adults there are some to whom the sign is
administered, rightly and properly in accordance with the
administration which God has committed to men, who do
not possess, either in the forum of conscience or in the forum
of the divine judgment, the inward grace of which baptism
is the sign. Yet this discrepancy does not preclude the administering of the ordinance to them so long as they fulfil
those conditions of intelligent and credible confession in reference to which men may judge. In like manner with respect
to infants the sign is properly dispensed in many cases where
the recipients do not possess and may never possess the inward
grace signified. It may be said that such are only in external
covenant relationship. But it may not be said that baptism
is simply the sign and seal of such external relationship.

3. The infant seed of those who are believers by confession
and profession should be baptised and thus bear the sign and
seal of the covenant of grace. This is the divine institution:
it is one of the ways by which it has pleased God to administer
the covenant of grace in the world; it is one of the ordinances
by means of which it pleases God to fulfil His covenant purposes from age to age and from generation to generation. It
is this fact of divine institution that constitutes the sufficient
ground for administering and receiving this ordinance. When
we ask the question: why do we baptise infants or upon what
ground do we dispense baptism to them? it is sufficient for
us to know and to answer that it is the divine institution.
God has ordained it as one of the provisions whereby He
administers His grace in the world. When the church prac-
tises this institution and complies with the divine command,
no further judgment respecting the secret purpose of God

nor respecting God's secret operations in the heart of those baptised is required as the proper *ground* upon which the ordinance is administered. To require any further information than the divine institution would go beyond the warrant of Scripture. It is true that in administering this ordinance we plead the promises which God has attached to faith and obedience, and we rest our faith and hope upon God's faithfulness. But our faith in God's promises would not appear to be placed in its proper relationship to infant baptism if it were conceived of as the *ground* for baptising infants. The ground is rather the institution which God has established and revealed, namely, that to the infant seed of believers the sign and seal of the covenant of grace is to be administered. Hence to aver that baptism is dispensed to infants on the ground of presumptive election or presumptive regeneration appears to be without warrant and also introduces perplexity into the question at issue.[30]

[30] Underlying this divine institution is the covenant administration which God has established in the world in pursuance of His redemptive purpose. God has ordained that the infant seed of believers be included in the covenant relation, and it is because infants are included that they receive the sign and seal of the covenant. In other words, the covenant of grace and the divinely instituted method of administering it in the world are the rationale of infant baptism. But when we are thinking specifically of the *ground* or *basis* upon which we act in administering baptism to infants it would seem necessary to focus attention upon the fact that it is the divine institution for the sign of the covenant to be given to the infant seed of the godly.

The notion of presumptive election appears in the First Helvetic Confession when, with reference to the baptism of infants it says, "praesertim quum de eorum electione pie est praesumendum" (Art. XXII). Charles Hodge adopts this notion. He says: "Since the promise is not only to parents but to their seed, children are, by the command of God, to be regarded and treated as of the number of the elect, until they give undeniable evidence to the contrary, or refuse to be so considered . . . It is not their vital union with Christ, nor their actual regeneration by the Holy Ghost, that is presumed, but their election . . . This presumption of election is not founded on their baptism, but their baptism is founded on this presumption" ("The Church Membership of Infants" in *The Biblical Repertory and Princeton Review*, 1858, pp. 375 f. n; *cf.* also pp. 377 f.). He contends that this is the doctrine of all the Reformed Churches and also claims it is the doctrine of Calvin, quoting from *Inst.* IV, xvi, 5, 6 in support of his claim.

Calvin in *Inst.* IV, xvi, 5–11 certainly holds that infants are baptised

In the case of adults we baptise on the basis of an intelligent
and credible confession, not on the basis of a judgment to the
effect that the person is regenerate and not even on the basis
of the judgment that the person is presumptively regenerate.
This is the divine ordinance. It is the institution of God that
all who make such a confession be baptised, and no further
judgment may be posited as the *ground* of the administration.
Likewise, in regard to infants, we baptise the infant seed of
those who make this confession simply because God has instituted this ordinance. Short of that we must not stop.
Beyond that we may not go.

This is not, of course, to say everything regarding the relations of those who are baptised to one another nor regarding

because the covenant belongs to them as to the infants of the Jews under
the Old Testament. Since they are partakers of the thing signified why
should they not receive the sign? The covenant remains in force and
includes infants. Baptism is now the mode of confirmation. "Let those,
therefore, who embrace the promise of God that he will perpetuate his
mercy to their offspring, consider it their duty to present them to the
Church to be signed with the symbol of mercy, and thereby to animate
their minds to stronger confidence, when they actually see the covenant
of the Lord engraven on the bodies of their children" (*Inst.* IV, xvi, 9).
It is without question, therefore, that Calvin regarded the inclusion
of believers' children in the covenant as the reason for the baptism of
such. To the present writer, however, this is not necessarily equivalent
to the statement of Hodge that infants are baptised because they are
presumptively elect or *presumptively* in the covenant. The reasons given
by Calvin for infant baptism appear to be rather closely adhered to in
the Second Helvetic Confession, Cap. XX, 6; The Heidelberg Catechism,
Q. 74; The French Confession, Art. XXXV; The Belgic Confession,
Art. XXXIV. The brevity of the statements in the British Confessions
is rather striking. The Thirty-Nine Articles say infant baptism is to
be retained "as most agreeable with the institution of Christ"; the Irish
Articles that it is to be retained "as agreeable to the Word of God";
the Westminster Confession that "the infants of one, or both, believing
parents, are to be baptized"; the Larger Catechism that "infants descending
from parents, either both, or but one of them, professing faith in Christ,
and obedience to him, are in that respect within the covenant, and to
be baptized"; the Shorter Catechism that "the infants of such as are
members of the visible church are to be baptized".
    B. B. Warfield uses the notion of presumptive membership in Christ's
body (*cf.* "The Polemics of Infant Baptism" in *Studies in Theology*,
New York, 1932, p. 390).
    For a historical survey and analysis see Lewis Bevens Schenck: *The
Presbyterian Doctrine of Children in the Covenant* (New Haven, 1940).

the attitude of the church to those baptised. Those making
the requisite confession and therefore baptised are to be received as believers, as those in union and communion with
Christ, and they are to be treated accordingly. Baptised
infants are to be received as the children of God and treated
accordingly.[31] But the proper ground of baptism, whether it
be that of adults or infants, consists in the divine institution
and command which regulate the church in these elements
of worship as in all others.

If we bear in mind these principles as they apply to the
divine method of administering the covenant of grace in the
world, we shall find ourselves in a better position to understand some of the instances which occur in Scripture and
which seem at first sight to confront us with great difficulty
and anomaly. These instances are specifically the circumcision of Ishmael and of Esau. Ishmael was certainly circumcised (Gen. 17:23) and we have every good reason to believe
that Esau was also. How could this be? The covenant was

[31] One of the finest statements on this subject is found in the Directory
for the Public Worship of God prepared by the Westminster Assembly.
Under the caption, "Of the Administration of the Sacraments" it reads:
"The seed and posterity of the faithful, born within the church have,
by their birth, interest in the covenant, and right to the seal of it. and
to the outward privileges of the church, under the gospel, no less than
the children of Abraham in the time of the Old Testament; the covenant
of grace, for substance, being the same; and the grace of God, and the
consolation of believers, more plentiful than before ... That children,
by baptism, are solemnly received into the bosom of the visible church,
distinguished from the world, and them that are without, and united
with believers; and that all who are baptized in the name of Christ, do
renounce, and by their baptism are bound to fight against the devil,
the world, and the flesh: That they are Christians, and federally holy
before baptism, and therefore are they baptized".
This evinces that the doctrine of the Westminster divines followed the
lines of thought enunciated by Calvin and formulated in such Reformed
creeds as the Belgic Confession and the Heidelberg Catechism, even
though the statements in the other Westminster Standards are brief and
do not show this so clearly.
If the word "presumptive" or its equivalent as used by the First Helvetic
Confession, Charles Hodge, and B. B. Warfield, for example, simply means
what the Directory, as quoted above, means, namely, that believers'
children are to be received as "Christians, and federally holy", then no
exception could be taken to its use. It is not certain, however, that this
is all that is implied in the use of such a notion as "presumptive election".

established with neither. If we think along the lines delineated above we shall see that the circumcision of Ishmael and of Esau is perfectly consonant with the divine method of administering the covenant in the world and provides us with the most instructive example of the application of this principle. The divinely prescribed principle of procedure was that all males should be circumcised, those born in the house or bought with money of any stranger (Gen. 17:12). The provisions of Genesis 17:9–14 are explicit to this effect. When these provisions are duly appreciated it will be recognised that for Abraham not to circumcise Ishmael and for Isaac not to circumcise Esau would have been a direct violation of the divine command. They were both circumcised. And they were circumcised in accordance with the principles of the divine institution as it was operative in the world. Circumcision was not withheld from them, for to withhold it from them would have been to act in accordance with other data of revelation *that did not regulate and were not intended to regulate the actual administration of the ordinance of circumcision.* To refrain from circumcising Ishmael and Esau would mean the importation and application of other data that did not provide the rule and that could not be interpreted as modifying the rule by which the covenant sign was to be administered. That rule was that *all* males should be circumcised.

It was prior to the circumcision of Ishmael that Abraham was told, "My covenant will I establish with Isaac". Rebecca knew by revelation, prior to the birth of her two sons, that Esau was to be rejected. But this information regarding the purpose of God could not properly be used either by Abraham or by Rebecca for depriving Ishmael or Esau respectively of the sign of circumcision. In accordance with the uniform principle enunciated in Genesis 17:9–14, circumcision was to be administered to all male children. In the case of Abraham we have in Genesis 17:21–23 the most eloquent witness to the fact that he did not fall into the error of confusing two things which must be kept distinct and therefore evidence of his sharp insight into the implications of the rule by which he was to be governed in the administering of the rite of circumcision. One of the outstanding features of Abraham's character was his unhesitating obedience to the revealed will of God. This appears in the very circumcision of Ishmael. Abraham had been commanded to circumcise all males, and this command he scrupulously obeyed. He did not regard the revelation that not in Ishmael would his seed be called as providing him with any warrant for suspension of this explicitly prescribed rule of procedure. We may presume that it was likewise in the case of Rebecca. The additional revelation of the purpose of God in reference to Esau could not properly be pleaded by her as a reason for depriving Esau of the sign of circumcision. Such withholding would have been contrary to the divine institution whereby she and Isaac were to govern their conduct in this matter. The circumcision of both Ishmael and Esau, when viewed in this light, is thoroughly consonant with the principles of procedure which governed the dispensing of this sign. And the same principles govern the dispensing of baptism to infants as well as to adults. Divine institution governs its administration. That is the *ground*. And that is what constitutes for us the obligation to comply.

Corroboratory Evidence

As was indicated already the evidence in support of infant baptism is not merely the absence of any repeal of the principle in accordance with which infants received the sign and seal of the covenant under the Old Testament. There is also the positive evidence which indicates that the same principle which gave meaning and validity to the circumcision of infants under the old economy is embedded and is operative in the administration of the covenant of grace under the new. This evidence is not of the nature of an express statute authorising the baptism of infants. There is no such statute. As we have seen, it would have been unnecessary, and that because of the organic unity and continuity of the covenant and of the church in both dispensations. The positive evidence is of a different sort, and this evidence is all the more significant precisely because it is of a different sort. It is evidence of the continued existence and operation of the principle without which infant circumcision and infant baptism would be little short of monstrosities. It is the principle of representation, of solidarity, of corporate relationship, coming to expression in the administration of God's redemptive and saving grace in the world. In other words, it is evidence that our Lord and his apostles taught and acted upon the recognition that the same principle which provided the basis of infant circumcision was to be applied in the administration of the kingdom of God and of the church.

1. *Matthew 18:1–6; 19:13, 14; Mark 9:36, 37; 10:14–16; Luke 18:15–17.*

It might readily be thought that when our Lord said, "Suffer the little children and forbid them not to come unto me, for of such is the kingdom of heaven" (Matt. 19:14; *cf.* Mark 10:14; Luke 18:16) he had in mind only such children as could come to Jesus of their own accord and were of sufficient age and understanding to answer to the description of Matthew 18:6, "these little ones who believe in me". Without determining the question as to the denotative scope of such an expression, it should be apparent that what Jesus says regarding the membership of little children in the kingdom of God cannot be restricted to children of sufficient age to be capable of intelligent understanding and faith. In Matthew 19:13 we are told that little children were brought to Jesus (*cf.* Mark 10:13) and the impression is distinctly created that the group included at least such as would not have come on their own initiative. All doubt, however, is removed by Luke 18:15, for there we are informed that the children were babes (βρέφη), that is to say, little infants. Hence our Lord's word to the effect that "of such is the kingdom of God" applies to little infants and not solely to children of more advanced years and intelligence.

Again, it might be supposed that when Jesus says, "Of such is the kingdom of God" all he means is that the kingdom of God is made up of those who are like little children and have a childlike spirit of simplicity and humility.[32] It is

---

[32] John Gill says: "The reason given for suffering little children to come to Christ; for of such is the kingdom of heaven, is to be understood in a figurative and metaphorical sense; of such who are comparable to children for modesty, meekness, and humility, and from freedom from rancour, malice, ambition and pride" (*op. cit.*, p. 295). Gill cites Calvin

true that in immediate connection with the statement concerned Jesus does say that "whosoever will not receive the
kingdom of God as a little child, he shall by no means enter
therein" (Mark 10:15; Luke 18:17; *cf.* Matt. 18:3). But we
are not to think that this is the import of the statement in
question, namely, "of such is the kingdom of God". What
Jesus is asserting here is rather that the kingdom of God
belongs to little children and that they are members of it,
not at all that the kingdom of God belongs to such as resemble little children. This can be shown by the following
considerations.

(a) The situation that evoked this disclosure on our Lord's
part was one in which little children as such are the centre of
interest. This is the case in all three passages where the
statement occurs (Matt. 19:13, 14; Mark 10:13–16; Luke
18:15–17). Little children were brought to the Lord that he
might touch them, lay his hands on them, and pray. The
disciples were forbidding this intrusion. Apparently they
thought that this was an unworthy interruption. Jesus was
moved with indignation. Why? Precisely because the disciples were forbidding the *little children* from being brought
and coming to him. It was then, and in specific reference to
that incident, that Jesus said, "Suffer the little children and
forbid them not to come unto me, for of such is the kingdom
of God". To suppose that our Lord was not speaking directly
of the little children and affirming their membership in the
kingdom of God would do plain violence to the actual facts
of the situation. It was with little children the disciples were
concerned, it was with little children Jesus was concerned,
the disciples to forbid them and Jesus to receive them. Little
children were in the focus of attention and interest, and it is
therefore of the little children themselves that Jesus proceeds
to speak.

as supporting this view of the clause in question. This is inaccurate.
What Calvin says in his comment on Matthew 19:14 is that "under
this term he (Jesus) includes both little children and those who resemble
them; for the Anabaptists foolishly exclude children, with whom the
subject must have commenced". Calvin clearly recognises that the clause
in question refers to the membership of infants in the kingdom of God
and not simply to the membership of those who resemble little children
in modesty and simplicity of spirit.

(b) When Jesus says, "Suffer the little children and forbid them not to come unto me", he is speaking of little children and not of those who are like little children in spirit and attitude. To say the least, it would be unnatural and harsh to suppose that the reason he appends to the exhortation would not have little children as its subject but another class of entirely different denotation. It should be seen that such an interpretation would not supply the proper reason for the exhortation, "Suffer the little children . . . to come unto me".[33]

(c) The demonstrative pronoun which is used points to the same conclusion. The pronoun (τοιοῦτος) means, "of this kind, sort, or class".[34] It is necessary to note the class of which Jesus had been speaking; it is distinctly and only of the infant class. This class alone provides us with the antecedent of the τοιούτων and not at all the class of those who are of childlike and humble spirit. Of the latter Jesus had not spoken. Neither were they in the focus of attention. The disciples were not forbidding such nor did Jesus here say of such, "Suffer them to come unto me".

The usage of the New Testament will show also that the force of τοιοῦτος is not to institute a comparison but rather to specify a class, and the class specified is defined by the context. In Matthew 18:5, for example, the expression, "one such little child" (ἓν παιδίον τοιοῦτο) is not "one illustrating the humble spirit" but "one such little child". Jesus is not saying, "Whoever will receive one like this little child in humility" but rather "one little child like this" (see also Mark 9:37). In John 4:23 the words, "The Father seeketh such to worship him" refer to those who worship in spirit and in truth and, obviously, not to those who are like such; the denotation is determined by the immediately preceding part of the verse. The following examples will verify this meaning and usage: John 9:36; Acts 19:25; 22:22; Romans 1:32; 16:18; I Corinthians 5:5; 7:15, 28; II Corinthians 2:7; 3:4; Galatians 5:21, 27; 6:1; Hebrews 7:26.

(d) The account of this incident given in Matthew 19:13, 14 has no reference to the childlike spirit requisite for entrance

---

[33] Cf. Calvin: Inst. IV, xvi, 7; Thomas Witherow: Scriptural Baptism — its Mode and Subjects, p. 56.

[34] Cf. Thomas Witherow: op. cit., pp. 56 f.

into the kingdom of heaven. Matthew, therefore, indicates that the statement, "Of such is the kingdom of heaven" was valid and was to be understood quite independently of any mention of the additional observation reported by Mark and Luke, namely, that whosoever will not receive the kingdom of God as a little child shall not enter therein.

We must conclude, therefore, that when Jesus says, "Of such is the kingdom of God" he is not speaking of the class resembling little children but is referring to little children themselves and affirms unmistakeably that little children are members of the kingdom of God. The thought expressed is not the quality which fits a person for entrance into the kingdom of God but rather the place which little children themselves are to have in the redemptive ministry of Jesus and their relation to the kingdom of God.

One further observation may be made regarding these passages. In Mark 9:41 the expression, "in my name" is explained by the qualifying clause, "because ye belong to Christ". To receive them in Christ's name is therefore equivalent to receiving them as belonging to Christ.[35] This, in turn, is but a variation of expression which has the same effect as saying that they belong to the kingdom of God.

To conclude: these two assertions — (1) that little children belong to the kingdom of God; (2) that they are to be received in Christ's name — do not offer stringent proof of infant baptism and they do not provide us with an express command to baptise infants. They do, however, supply us with certain principles which lie close to the argument for infant baptism and without which the ordinance of infant baptism would be meaningless. These principles are: (1) that little children, even infants, are among Christ's people and are members of his body; (2) that they are members of his kingdom and therefore have been regenerated; (3) that they belong to the church, in that they are to be received as belonging to Christ, that is to say, received into the fellowship of the saints. The force of all this is greatly enhanced when we remember the occasion of Jesus' assertion, "of such is the kingdom of God". The attitude of the disciples, to which these words of Jesus were the rebuke, was one that rested on the

35 Cf. ibid. p. 53.

assumption that little children were not of sufficient importance to occupy the attentions of Jesus and were not really within the compass of his kingdom task. In contrast, our Lord's reply is to the effect that none are more intimately involved in his redemptive work and ministry than little infants and that therefore they are to be received into the bosom of the saints' fellowship and love. If little children belong to the kingdom of God, if they belong to Christ, if they are to be received into the fellowship of believers, if they are to be reckoned as possessing the qualities and rights that constitute them members of the kingdom of God and of the church, is there any reason why they should not receive the sign of that membership? In fact it would appear to be the proper and necessary recognition of that which the Lord himself explicitly asserted and of the injunction he so emphatically gave to his disciples. Surely the inference is one of good and necessary consequence that infants should be given the sign and seal of that which, by the authority of Christ, they are to be accounted. There is nothing signified and sealed by baptism that is in excess of that which our Lord asserts infants to be and of that which he commands they should be accounted.

Obviously this does not apply to all little children. And it does not of itself settle the mooted question of the fate of infants dying in infancy. Such applications were ostensibly outside the universe of discourse. The statements of our Lord with reference to the membership of infants in the kingdom of God can be applied only to such little children as come within the compass of a covenant situation analogous to that in which our Lord's words were spoken. Any universalising of the assertion would violate the most elementary canons of proper interpretation.

2. *Ephesians 6:1, 4; Colossians 3:20, 21.*

In these passages the apostle Paul includes the children among those who are addressed as saints. In the contexts of both passages exhortations are being given to the various classes of saints — wives, husbands, fathers, servants, masters. The exhortation in each case is appropriate to the specific duty and particular station of each class. It should also be noted that in each case the apostle frames and directs his exhortation in terms of the Christian standing and character of the persons concerned. He is addressing wives, husbands, fathers, servants, masters as believers in Christ and as those therefore who recognise their allegiance to Christ as Lord. It is in such a context that children, as constituting one particular class among others, are exhorted to cultivate the specific virtue appropriate to them. It is necessary, therefore, to understand that the children are reckoned as saints in terms of the salutation in both epistles and that they are not regarded as belonging to any different category in respect of the Saviourhood and Lordship of Christ. Everything points to the conclusion that children, equally with parents and servants and masters, belong to the body of Christ and are fully embraced in the fellowship of the saints. If children were thus recognised and received in the apostolic churches, they were recognised as possessing the status of which baptism is the sign and seal. If this is so, there is no reason why such children should not have received the sign and seal of their status and privilege.

3. I Corinthians 7:14.

Apparently believers in Corinth who found themselves in the anomalous situation of being united in wedlock with unbelieving partners were afraid that their Christian standing and character would be prejudiced by this mixed marital relationship. The apostle was writing to encourage them against this fear. The encouragement he provides is that the unbelieving husband is sanctified in the wife and the unbelieving wife is sanctified in the brother. In order to reinforce the argument drawn from this principle he appeals to what had been apparently recognised among the Corinthians, namely, that the children of even one believing parent were not unclean but rather holy.[36] That is the force of the statement "Else were your children unclean, but now are they holy". It is quite striking that the apostle does not feel called upon to vindicate or establish this truth; it was taken for granted

---

[36] Cf. B. B. Warfield: op. cit., pp. 397 f.; Thomas Witherow: op. cit., pp. 53 ff. John Gill regards the holiness spoken of in this passage as that merely of "legitimate marriage and offspring" (op. cit., p. 304).

and therefore without argument pleaded as the premise already conceded by the Corinthians. This shows that the sanctification of the children of parents, only one of whom was a believer, was a recognised principle in the apostolic tradition. It is this principle, clearly enunciated in I Corinthians 7:14, that underlies the ordinance of infant baptism. It does not, of course, offer stringent proof of infant baptism. But it does show that the children of a believer are not in the same category, in respect of "sanctification", as the children who have no Christian parentage. There is a status or condition that can be characterised as "holiness", which belongs to children in virtue of a parental relationship.

In view of the context we cannot maintain that this "holiness" is that of regeneration. But it can be nothing less than the "holiness" of connection and privilege. It is a "holiness" that evinces the operation of the covenant and representative principle and proves that the Christian faith of even one parent involves the embrace of the offspring in a relationship that is by divine warrant described as "holy". This is wholly consonant with the basis upon which the ordinance of infant baptism rests, just as it is counter to the moving principle of the antipaedobaptist contention.

4. *Acts 16:15, 33, 34; I Cor. 1:16 (cf. Acts 10:47, 48; 11:14).*

These are the instances of household baptism. We cannot prove conclusively that there were infants in these households. But the significance of such explicit reference to the baptism of households appears when we take into account two considerations. There is, first of all, the fact that there are relatively few instances of actual baptism recorded in the New Testament.[37] It is remarkable that there should be so few.

---

[37] The reference here, of course, is to actual instances of Christian baptism. *Cf.* in this connection Thomas Witherow: *op. cit.*, pp. 57 f. When John Gill says, for example, "it is strange, exceeding strange, that among the many thousands baptized in Jerusalem, Samaria, Corinth, and other places, that there should be no one instance of any of them bringing their children with them to be baptized, and claiming the privilege of baptism for them upon their own faith; nor of their doing this in any short time after" (*op. cit.*, p. 306), he is not taking proper account of

We should expect that there would be a very large number. For actual baptism must have been very frequent in the days of the apostles. But only some twelve instances are actually recorded (Acts 2:41; 8:12, 13, 38; 9:18; 10:48; 16:15, 33; 18:8; 19:5, I Cor. 1:14, 16). It is quite illuminating that at least three of these instances refer to household baptism. Every consideration would point to the conclusion that household baptism was a frequent occurrence in the practice of the church in the apostolic days. If so, it would be practically impossible to believe that in none of these households were there any infants. It would be unreasonable to believe so. The infants in the households belonged to the households and would be baptised. Presumption is, therefore, of the strongest kind, even though we do not have an overt and proven instance of infant baptism. There is, in the second place, the representative principle which is embedded in the Scripture and is woven into the warp and woof of the administration of grace in the world. When we appreciate this we can understand how readily the apostles would apply this principle in the dispensing of the ordinances of grace. Household baptism would be a perfectly natural application.[38] And this would inevitably involve the baptism of the infants comprised in the household whenever and wherever there were such.

the fewness of references to actual baptism. He is building an argument upon the numbers baptised, when what is relevant to the question is not the numbers actually baptised but the number of times in the New Testament in which there is reference to the actual administration of the rite.

[38] In connection with household baptism reference might also be made to the absence of any evidence of the baptism of adults who were born of Christian parents and who were brought up in a Christian household. Paedobaptists have appealed to this consideration as providing at least presumptive evidence in favour of the belief that in apostolic practice the children of believers were baptised in infancy. Most recently, Oscar Cullmann in his booklet *Die Tauflehre des Neuen Testaments* (Zurich, 1948) presses this consideration rather strongly. He says, for example: "Those who dispute the Biblical character of infant Baptism have therefore to reckon with the fact that *adult Baptism for sons and daughters born of Christian parents, which they recommend, is even worse attested by the New Testament than infant baptism* (for which certain possible traces are discoverable) *and indeed lacks any kind of proof*" (p. 21; Eng. Trans. by J. K. S. Reid, *Baptism in the New Testament* (Chicago, 1950), p. 26).

5. *Acts 2:38, 39.*

The relevance of this text concerns the clause in verse 39, "For the promise is to you and to your children". There is no room for question that the children are coordinated with the adults who are being addressed by Peter on this occasion. And the important consideration is that the promise, which is urged as an incentive to, or reason for, repentance and baptism, stands in the same relation to the children as to the adults being addressed. This is the force of the coordination.

It might be argued that the children being contemplated here are simply and solely those of age and intelligence sufficient for the intelligent repentance urged in the preceding verse. Or it might be said that the children come into the purview of the passage and therefore within the purview of the promise only as they attain to an age of understanding which will make them capable of such repentance and also of the call referred to in the latter part of the verse. On this interpretation the promise could not be conceived of as actually embracing infants or young children. But there is nothing in the text to indicate that there is such restriction in the denotation of the children referred to. And it would be entirely counter to everything in the revelation which formed the background of Peter's statement and which provided the basis of it. We may well ask: what was there in the revelation of the Old Testament or in the teaching of Jesus which would give the least support or even plausibility to the supposition that in the denotation of those designated "children" a line of distinction must be drawn between little infants and grownups? To institute such discrimination would be the resort of desperation, would be without any warrant in the context of Scripture and would be contrary to the analogy of Scripture usage. Hence we must believe that the children spoken of are the children of those being addressed, and as the children of such they are for that reason placed in the same category as their parents in reference to the promise. Simply stated this means that the promise is to the children as well as to the parents and that, in respect of this property, the children are included with their parents.

We are not in a position to appreciate the significance of this unless we bear in mind the covenant relation established by God and clearly revealed in the Old Testament. It is in the light of Genesis 17:7, "And I will establish my covenant between me and thee and thy seed after thee throughout their generations for an everlasting covenant, to be a God unto thee and to thy seed after thee" (cf. Deut. 29:10–13) that this word of Peter is to be understood. It is this principle, institution, or arrangement alone that gives meaning to Peter's appeal.

Now, what does this imply? It demonstrates that Peter, in the illumination and power of the Spirit of Pentecost, recognised that there was no suspension or abrogation of that divine administration whereby children are embraced with their parents in God's covenant promise. It is simply this and nothing less that Acts 2:39 evinces. Pentecost is to be coordinated with the incarnation, death, and resurrection of Christ as one of the epochal events in the economy of redemption. We may well regard Pentecost as that which brought to fruition the inauguration of the new dispensation. Nothing could advertise more conspicuously and conclusively that this principle of God's gracious government, by which children along with their parents are the possessors of God's covenant promise, is fully operative in the New Testament as well as in the Old than this simple fact that on the occasion of Pentecost Peter took up the refrain of the old covenant and said, "The promise is to you and to your children". It is the certification of the Holy Spirit to us that this method of the administration of the covenant of grace is not suspended.

It is precisely because there is such evidence of the perpetual operation of this gracious principle in the administration of God's covenant that we baptise infants. It is for that reason alone that we continue to baptise them. It is the divine institution, not, indeed, commended by human wisdom and not palatable to those who are influenced by the dictates of human wisdom, yet commended by the wisdom of God. It is the seal to us of His marvellous goodness that He is not only a God to His people but also to their seed after them.

V

Objections to Infant Baptism

Some of the objections to infant baptism have been antici-
pated in the earlier parts of our discussion and the answers to
such objections are implicit in the argument already presented.
It may be necessary, however, to bring these objections into
clearer focus and deal with them more directly. There are
also other objections which have not been considered so far
and which require some examination.

1. One of the most persuasive objections and one which
closes the argument for a great many people is that there is
no express command to baptise infants and no record in the
New Testament of a clear case of infant baptism. In answering
such an objection there is no denial of the propositions made
in the objection. It is only too apparent that if we had an
express command or even a proven case with apostolic sanc-
tion, then the controversy would not have arisen; at least
it would be of a very different sort. The answer to this objection is simply the reminder that an express command or a
proven instance is not the only kind of evidence that should
be regarded as sufficient. What by good and necessary inference can be deduced from Scripture is of authority in the
church of God as well as what is expressly set down in Scripture. The evidence for infant baptism falls into the category
of good and necessary inference, and it is therefore quite
indefensible to demand that the evidence required must be
in the category of express command or explicit instance. In
other words, the assumption upon which this objection rests
is a false assumption and one which cannot be adopted as
the norm in determining what Christian doctrine or Christian
institution is.

In reference to this objection it is necessary to be reminded
again how few instances there are in the New Testament of
the actual dispensing of the ordinance of Christian baptism
This places the silence regarding an overt reference to infant

baptism in a very different light. And it also accords to the three explicit references to household baptism a significance which we might not readily detect. Although there are only three instances recorded, analogy would require us to believe that household baptism was quite common. It would be unreasonable to suppose that there were no infants in these many households, and if there were infants they were included in the household baptised.

2. It is objected that the instances we have of baptism presuppose a credible and intelligent profession of faith and therefore something of which infants are incapable. It is not by any means apparent that this objection, even as a proposition, rests upon solid ground. For who is to assure us that when households were baptised every one receiving baptism was required to make an intelligent and credible profession of faith? The very proposition, therefore, is not proven.

But even if we allow for the element of truth which there is in the objection, namely, that in most cases actually referred to the dispensing of baptism is attached to the demand for repentance and faith, the objection is not a valid one. The exhortation of Peter on the day of Pentecost that his hearers should be baptised in the name of Jesus Christ was certainly coordinated with the appeal for repentance (Acts 2:38). And the baptism of the Philippian jailor by Paul followed upon the appeal, "Believe upon the Lord Jesus" and the speaking to him the Word of God (Acts 16:31–33). But these and like instances do not settle the question at issue. Such preaching and administration of baptism presuppose the presence of adults, and it is not a matter of dispute that where adults are being baptised there must be the demand for repentance and faith and a credible confession. It does not follow that infants, who in the nature of the case are not capable of making such confession, are ineligible for baptism.[39] It no more follows that infants are excluded than does it follow that they are excluded from salvation. In the case of adults intelligent repentance and faith are the conditions of salvation. But intelligent repentance and faith are not the conditions of

---

[39] Cf. Calvin: *Inst.* IV, xvi, 19–29; Peter Williams: *Candid Reasons for Renouncing the Principles of Antipaedobaptism* (Edinburgh, 1876), pp. 24 ff.; Thomas Witherow: *op. cit.*, pp. 37 ff.

salvation in the case of infants. They are not psychologically capable of such faith and its corresponding confession. It is so in reference to baptism. In the case of adults the demand of repentance and faith in order to baptism is mandatory. The instances which are adduced by the opponents of infant baptism could have relevance only where adults were concerned. But they can have no relevance to the case of infants who cannot be the subjects of such preaching and of the demand for repentance which accompanies it.

3. It can be objected that we have no way of knowing whether or not infants are regenerate, whether or not they are members of Christ's body. It is, admittedly, quite true that we have no way of inquiring into the subjective spiritual state of little infants. But the objection based on this fact has no validity. Baptism is not dispensed on the basis of our knowledge that the person concerned is regenerate. This is not true even in the case of adults. In accordance with divine institution the ordinance is administered to those who make an intelligent and credible profession of faith. In the case of infants it is administered on the basis of the divine institution and not on the basis of a prerogative which the present objection assumes.

4. It is objected that infants cannot understand the meaning of that which is dispensed. Of course they cannot. But that they derive no benefit from baptism or that it is not the divine method of signifying and sealing blessing to them is by no means a proper inference. The same objection would apply to circumcision and would impinge upon the wisdom and grace of God who instituted it. The same objection, if valid, would apply to Christ's blessing of little infants. This objection, in fact, rests upon the iniquitous assumption that all blessing is contingent upon conscious understanding of its import on our part. Are we to say, for example, that it is of no avail to the infant to be born and nurtured in a Christian family simply because the infant has no conscious understanding of the great blessing that belongs to him in the care, protection, devotion, and nurture of Christian parents? Is it of no significance to the infant to be "laid in Christ's way" simply because the infant does not yet know that to be the case? And to aver that to be baptised into the name of the Father, and of the Son, and of the Holy Ghost can have little

or no meaning because the infant does not know the meaning is utterly to misconstrue the nature of God's grace and of His institutions. The means of grace are the channels along which the saving and sanctifying grace of God flows. To be in the channel of grace by God's appointment is of deepest consequence. It is only worldly-wise calculation and not reasoning inspired by the recognition of the methods of divine grace that can find any force in this type of objection.

5. It may appear to be an argument of some weight to appeal to the sad record of so many who have been baptised in infancy — they have grown up to be indifferent to the baptismal engagements and have often lived lives of infidelity and godlessness. This record is not denied. The sad truth is to be deplored. But perversion and abuse are never proper arguments against an institution. The perversion of the best is the worst. This objection tells as much against adult baptism as against infant baptism. Many baptised on their own confession have proven unfaithful and have lived godless lives.

What this record does prove is the necessity of appreciating the great truth that the institutions of grace always carry with them their responsibilities and obligations. Too often those who are the beneficiaries of this institution of grace rest upon the institution rather than upon the God whose administration it is. Hence the moral and spiritual catastrophes of Christian history.

6. It is objected that the argument drawn from circumcision is not valid because of the great discrepancy that exists between circumcision and baptism.[40] The difference between the import of circumcision and that of baptism is not at all what is claimed to be the case. It has been shown already that there is an essential identity of meaning, an identity confirmed by the New Testament itself (*cf.* Col. 2:11, 12). The force of the objection might, however, appear to take on a good deal of plausibility when we are reminded that circumcision was administered only to males, whereas in baptism such discrimination between male and female is obliterated. It is true that only males were circumcised. Why a sign and seal had been selected under the Old Testament which could be dispensed only to males it is not our present interest to determine. This was the divine institution. It is,

<hr />

[40] *Cf.* John Gill: *op. cit.*, pp. 298 ff.

however, altogether consonant with the extension of grace and the expansion of privilege revealed in the New Testament that a sign should be chosen in the new economy that could be dispensed to females just as well as to males. Is it not one of the glories of the New Testament that there is now in Christ Jesus no longer male nor female, just as there is no longer Jew nor Gentile, bond nor free, barbarian nor Scythian? And it is consonant with the contrasted relative restrictions of the Old Testament that only males should bear this covenant sign and seal. But this difference in no way affects the fact that circumcision was the sign and seal of the covenant of God's grace under the Old Testament, that it was dispensed to infants, that this administration implied that infants were embraced with their parents in the covenant favour of God, that this is an established principle in the economy of divine grace, that baptism takes the place of circumcision as the sign and seal of the covenant, and that the administering of baptism to infants stands in the most intimate relation to the administering of circumcision to them under the Old Testament. The differences as well as the similarities bespeak, and are consonant with, the sum total of factors which have to be taken into account as we unfold the relationships that exist between the two Testaments.

7. It is objected that paedobaptists are strangely inconsistent in dispensing baptism to infants and yet refusing to admit them to the Lord's table. The supposed analogy of the passover might appear to give added point to this objection and the inconsistency of paedobaptists made more blatant. Under the Old Testament, it may be said, infants were circumcised and partook of the passover. Under the New Testament Baptists exclude infants from both of the corresponding ordinances, baptism and the Lord's supper. Exclusion from the former is consonant with exclusion from the latter. And exclusion from the Lord's supper indicates the cleavage that exists in this matter between the Old Testament and the New, a cleavage exemplified also in the exclusion of infants from baptism in contradistinction from the Old Testament under which they received circumcision. On the other hand, paedobaptists appeal to Old Testament circumcision in support of the argument for infant baptism but

abandon the analogy of the Old Testament completely when it comes to the Lord's supper.

The fallacy of this kind of argument, as far as the passover is concerned, resides in the assumption that little infants partook of the passover. There is no evidence that this was the case. It would be unreasonable to think that they did; the diet was hardly suitable for infants. That children when they grew up and were able to ask: "what mean ye by this service?" and were able to understand its meaning partook of the passover is altogether likely. But children of such age and intelligence are in a different category from infants. Paedobaptists do not refuse to admit to the Lord's table children of sufficient age and understanding to know the meaning of the Lord's supper.

But the main point of the objection needs to be considered on its own merits, quite apart from the argument respecting the passover. Why baptise infants if we do not admit them to the Lord's table?

At the outset it should be admitted that if paedobaptists are inconsistent in this discrimination, then the relinquishment of infant baptism is not the only way of resolving the inconsistency. It could be resolved by going in the other direction, namely, that of admitting infants to the Lord's supper. And when all factors entering into this dispute are taken into account, particularly the principle involved in infant baptism, then far less would be at stake in admitting infants to the Lord's supper than would be at stake in abandoning infant baptism. This will serve to point up the significance of infant baptism in the divine economy of grace.

It does not, however, follow that there is the inconsistency alleged. The following considerations show that there are distinctions between the Lord's supper and baptism which make it reasonable, to say the least, that the one should be dispensed to infants and the other not.

(a) Baptism signifies and seals what lies at the basis and inception of a state of salvation, to wit, union with Christ, cleansing from the pollution of sin, and cleansing from the guilt of sin. It signifies what infants may possess as well as adults and must possess in order to be in a state of salvation.

(b) The Lord's supper, on the other hand, signifies something that is consequent upon the state of salvation. It presupposes that which is sealed by baptism. The two central significations of the Lord's supper are commemoration and communion. Commemoration implies the recognition of Christ as our Saviour who died for us, communion the recognition that he as our resurrected and living Saviour is present with us and seals that presence in the elements of bread and wine. The notions associated with the Lord's supper, such as remembrance, communion, discerning of the Lord's body, are of such a nature that they involve conscious intelligent understanding. It is surely reasonable to infer that such intelligent exercise of heart and mind belongs to the essence of that which the Lord's supper contemplates.[41] And, if so, it is sharply distinguished from that signified and sealed by baptism.

(c) Baptism represents something that is performed once for all and is not repeated. The fruits and blessings of that which is represented are permanent and ever-increasing. But the grace represented is unrepeatable. This is why baptism is dispensed only once.

(d) It is otherwise with the Lord's supper. It represents what is daily repeated in the life of the believer. Hence the Lord's supper is to be received frequently.

(e) It is far from irrelevant to observe the difference between baptism and the Lord's supper in respect of the elements used and the actions involved. Baptism is washing with water, something necessary and appropriate to the infant in the earliest stages of life. There is nothing in the element or the action incongruous with earliest infancy. The Lord's supper is the partaking of bread and wine. We can readily

---

[41] The objection on the part of antipaedobaptists, to the effect that the exercise of intelligent understanding required in the partaking of the Lord's supper is entirely parallel to that required on the part of adults in the case of baptism and therefore cannot be consistently pleaded by paedobaptists as a reason for excluding infants from the Lord's supper any more than it can be pleaded as a reason for excluding them from baptism, is not valid. What is being pleaded is that the very things signified by the Lord's supper involve intelligent understanding on the part of the participant. The things signified by baptism, however, do not necessarily involve intelligent understanding, and baptism may therefore be administered to those who are incapable of such understanding. The parallelism which antipaedobaptists plead is apparent and not real.

detect that there is in the elements used and the actions involved something that is not congruous with early infancy. To say the least, we encounter a difficulty is dispensing the Lord's supper to infants that is not even suggested in the case of baptism.

In all of this we see a striking parallelism between the sealing ordinances of the Old and New Testaments. Without reiterating all the points of resemblance, suffice it to be reminded that circumcision was administered to infants; it was administered only once; it was appropriate to infants; it was the rite of initiation; there is no evidence that infants partook of the passover; the diet was not appropriate to their age; the passover was repeated each year.

Summarily stated, baptism represents the inclusion of the person baptised in the body of Christ and in the fellowship of the saints — it is the rite that signifies initiation; the Lord's supper represents the abiding responsibility of and provision for those who are the members of Christ's body — it is the rite of edification.

We see, therefore, that there is a series of considerations wholly consonant with the practice of paedobaptists when they dispense baptism to infants and exclude them from the Lord's supper. The diversity in the ordinances warrants the discrimination in practice. Instead of being charged with inconsistency we should rather claim that the practice of paedobaptists reflects the considerations which inhere in the nature and characteristics of the respective ordinances.

VI

Whose Children
are to be Baptised?

The question raised in the above caption is very largely the question: what parents are eligible to receive baptism for their children? In dealing with this question it is necessary to be reminded again of the distinction between the terms in which the church must be defined, on the one hand, and the prerogative which belongs to men in the divinely instituted administration exercised by them, on the other. In the forum of conscience and in the forum of divine judgment only those united to Christ and who are members of his body have a right to present their children for baptism. The basis of infant baptism is the covenant relation which God has established with his people and the covenant relationship which the children of such sustain to God by His own institution. Those who are not in covenant with God cannot claim any of the rights and privileges which belong to the covenant. This needs to be emphasised in order to obviate a good many of the errors which have distorted or perplexed thinking on this subject. Only those united to Christ in the virtue of his death and in the efficacy and power of his resurrection have a right before God to claim the promises of the covenant of grace; only such can claim the privilege which God bestows upon their children and the promises He gives in respect of them to His covenant people.

We are now interested, however, more particularly in the criteria which are to be applied by men in the administration of this ordinance, the criteria by which men are to judge in the administration which God has committed to them. Since baptism is the sign and seal of union with Christ and of membership in his body the church, it scarcely needs to be said that the *sine qua non* of eligibility is that the parents them-

selves must have been baptised. The basis of infant baptism
is the covenant relationship which God has established. If
parents are not willing to avow this covenant and receive its
sign and seal, it would be mockery for them to present their
children for baptism on the basis of a covenant institution
which they do not acknowledge. Only baptised parents may
present their children for baptism.

Baptised parents are, however, of two kinds, those baptised
in infancy and those baptised as adults on the basis of personal confession of faith. In the case of the latter it is apparent
that their baptism presupposes an intelligent and credible
confession of faith, and so, when they present their children
for baptism, there is not only the antecedent of their own
baptism but also the confession of faith prerequisite to it.
Hence, in their case, there are in reality two prerequisites,
confession of faith and baptism. But how is it in the case of
those who have been baptised in infancy? No personal confession of faith preceded their baptism. Are they to receive
baptism for their children on the ground that they themselves
have been baptised and on that ground alone, that is to say,
on the ground of their confederate membership in the church?

It should be understood that the mere fact of baptism in
infancy does not entitle the persons thus baptised to any of
the privileges of the church of Christ if, when they come to
years of discretion and understanding, they show no interest in covenant responsibilities and privileges. If they are
indifferent and walk contrary to the gospel they are to be
disciplined accordingly, and one of the ways in which such
discipline would be exercised is the denial to them of the
privilege of baptism for their children until they repent and
amend their ways. Confederate members of the church, it
should be remembered, are under the discipline of the church.
Too frequently this is forgotten. Neither they themselves nor
the church may proceed on the assumption that they are
immune to discipline until they become communicant members. But, while it is conceded that baptised members who
contradict their covenant engagements by a life and walk
contrary to the gospel are not eligible to receive baptism for
their children, what of those who have been baptised in
infancy, and are outwardly circumspect in their lives and

attentive upon the means of grace? May they receive baptism for their children simply on the basis of their confederate membership in the church? Or are they also required to make public confession of faith in Christ as their Saviour and Lord, a confession equivalent to that which would be required if they were receiving baptism for themselves?

Such a question ought to remind us again that confederate members of the church as well as communicant members are under the supervision and discipline of the church. If the church is vigilant and faithful, confederate members will be constantly under the instruction of the church and, ordinarily, long before they have children of their own, will be confronted with their covenant responsibilities and privileges. They will be advised that the necessary implicate of the covenant relation, sealed by their baptism in infancy, is the open avowal and embrace of that covenant and the public confession of Christ as their only Saviour and Lord. To deny this logical necessity is to make mockery of the covenant that is sealed by baptism. If, therefore, confederate members are not ready or willing to embrace the covenant grace sealed by baptism and not willing to make the confession incident to it, then they are liable to discipline and, obviously, they are not in a fit state to receive baptism for their children. Confession of faith is involved, therefore, in the very avowal of the covenant which is presupposed in the presentation of children for baptism.

In speaking of the discipline which is exercised over confederate members, and particularly when they come to years of understanding or maturity, it should be understood that there is no stereotyped pattern of discipline. Each case must be dealt with on its merits, and great patience and prudence as well as faithfulness must be exercised in bringing people to a realisation of what is entailed in the baptismal covenant. There is the danger of formal confession without meaning, and there is also the danger of undue hesitation and delay. But that confession of faith is the condition of receiving baptism for our children inheres in the very logic of the covenant relation. The presentation of children for baptism implies avowal of the covenant, an avowal which implies confession, and this surely requires that those who are charged with the administration should insure that the confession is intelligent and consistent. Sufficient has already been said to show that the confession in view can be nothing less than a confession of faith in Jesus as Saviour and Lord, that is to say, a confession of true faith and not merely of intellectual or historical faith. It is a confession of faith that corresponds to that of which baptism is the sign and seal, namely, union with Christ and membership in his body the church.

There remains the question, which has often been a burning one: what is the relation of communicant membership to eligibility for the reception of baptism for infants? It is apparent that the confession required for the reception of baptism for infants is the confession which makes the persons concerned eligible for communicant membership. It is a great fallacy and one fraught with grave consequence to suppose that there is such a thing in the New Testament as dual confession, one entitling to baptism and another, of a higher order, entitling to communicant membership.[42] There is no

[42] William Cunningham has reflected ably and cogently on this fallacy which he regarded as a growing evil in his day. He says: "So far as concerns the subjects of the sacraments . . . it is generally admitted, that partaking in the Lord's Supper implies a profession of faith in Christ, and is therefore warrantable and beneficial only to believers. But many, and we fear a growing number, refuse to admit this principle as applicable to baptism. It is contended, not only that infants who are incapable of faith ought to be baptised . . . but also that adults may be admitted to baptism, though they are not, and do not profess to be, believers and regenerate persons, — baptism, it is alleged, not expressing or implying a profession of believing in Christ, but only a profession of willingness to be instructed in the principles of Christianity. This notion is flatly opposed to the leading views with respect to the sacraments which have always prevailed in the Protestant churches, and been embodied in the Reformed confessions . . . The attempt to make so wide a gulf between baptism and the Lord's Supper, and to extend the application of baptism beyond the range of the membership of the church, so as to include all who are placed, by their own voluntary act, or that of their parents, under the church's superintendence and instruction, while neither in connection with their own baptism nor that of their children are they held to make a profession of faith and regeneration, is, of course, flatly opposed to the definition or description of a sacrament, given in the confessions of the Reformed churches as applicable to both ordinances. It is also, we are persuaded, inconsistent with every consideration suggested by the symbolic or emblematic character of the ordinance as an outward act, implying

warrant for such dualism in our conception of confession. Hence it should be accepted as incontrovertible that the confession made in baptism, whether it be our own baptism or the baptism of our children, is the confession required for communicant membership. Those making this confession should be admitted, and should consider themselves as obligated to come, to the Lord's table. But what of those who, nevertheless, refrain from coming? May they be denied baptism for their children until they do come?

Here again each case must be dealt with on its own merits. There is no stereotyped pattern of treatment. It is easy to envisage cases in which persons making a thoroughly satisfactory confession might receive baptism for their children before the actual opportunity might present itself for them to carry their confession to its logical result by partaking of the Lord's supper. It would be unduly harsh to require in such cases that the baptism of their infants should be postponed until the opportunity would present itself for them to partake of communion. By confession they are received to communicant membership, and it should be taken for granted that they will fulfil that obligation when the opportunity arrives. In the meantime they may receive baptism for their infants.

But the situation is more complex where there is the refusal to partake of the Lord's supper, and especially where this refusal is persistent and prolonged. The confession made for the reception of baptism is a confession of faith in Christ as Saviour and of fidelity to him as Lord. Such a confession clearly implies the obligation to obey Christ's commands and, specifically in this connection, the command to commemorate his dying love, "This do in remembrance of me". Persistent refusal to fulfil the implicate of the Christian confession subjects the person to the discipline of the church. It would be inconsistent with the requirements of discipline to ignore the sin of disobedience to Christ's command. One of the inevitable

a declaration or profession of a certain state of mind and feeling on the part of the person baptized, and with all that is asserted or indicated in Scripture as to the connection between baptism on the one hand, and remission and regeneration on the other" ("Zwingle and the Doctrine of the Sacraments", *op. cit.*, pp. 268 ff.).

measures of discipline to be exercised in such a case would be
to deny to the persons involved the privilege of baptism for
their children.

Again it needs to be said, however, that every case must
be dealt with on its own merits. Among those who refrain
from the Lord's supper there is much diversity. Some are
careless and indifferent and they must be dealt with according
to the character of their perversity. Some may be afflicted
with a spurious piety that underestimates the significance of
the ritual observed in the Lord's supper. They must be dealt
with in a different way. Some are imbued with a wholesome
tenderness and deep sense of the solemnity of the Lord's
supper. Such must be encouraged, and instructed to understand that the Lord's supper is for all who love the Lord in
sincerity and truth, that the Lord's supper is not for the elite
of believers but for the weak as well as for the strong.

The severity of discipline, therefore, must be proportionate
to the gravity of the offense. And in judging the gravity of
the offense all the circumstances and conditions must be taken
into account. The general principle, however, must hold that
the confession required for the baptism of our infants is of
such a character that obedience to Christ's dying command is
one of its implications. And where such obedience is absent
the disobedient makes himself or herself ineligible for the
enjoyment of the privileges which follow upon the confession.
Not the least of these privileges is the baptism of infant
offspring.

VII

The Efficacy of Baptism

The rite of baptism consists in washing with water in the name of the Father, and of the Son, and of the Holy Ghost. It involves, therefore, the use of a visible element and an observable action. The meaning of this washing with water is that it signifies and seals a spiritual fact or relationship, namely, union with Christ and membership in his body the church. What efficacy attaches to this observable action?

It is apparent that as a sign or seal it should not be identified with that which is signified and sealed. That which signifies is not the thing signified and that which seals is not the thing sealed. The sign or seal presupposes the existence of that which is signified or sealed. Hence baptism is the sign and seal of a spiritual reality which is conceived of as existing. Where that reality is absent the sign or seal has no efficacy.[43]

Equally pertinent is the observation that the sign or seal does not bring into existence that which is signified or sealed. It does not effect union with Christ. In other words, baptism does not convey or confer the grace which it signifies.[44] Bap-

[43] It is not being forgotten that the administration of baptism, in addition to the proclamation of the gospel, is one way in which God declares and certifies to us the truth of the gospel. The dispensing of baptism even in the presence of unbelievers has, therefore, a teaching and witnessing ministry and brings vividly to the attention of those who are without Christ our sinful condition, the provision of the gospel, and the high privilege of union with Christ. Both sacraments may be said to have this efficacy of bringing home to the ungodly what the gospel is. They should always be dispensed in connection with the preaching of the Word and in such coordination they serve to enforce the gospel. But this kind of efficacy is not the subject with which we are now dealing. The question is the efficacy of baptism in reference to those to whom it is dispensed.

[44] This is directed against the notion of baptismal regeneration. It hardly seems necessary to set forth any extended refutation of this sacerdotalist conception. It has been ably dealt with by various

tism is a means of grace but not a means of conferring the
grace represented. It is a means of grace to signify and
confirm grace. The notion that it is the instrument of be-
stowing the grace or of constituting the fact signified is
contrary to the nature of the rite as a sign and seal.

What precisely is its efficacy? It might be argued that if
the grace it signifies or seals is presupposed, what need is
there for this ordinance? Is not the grace of God sufficiently
real and secure in itself apart from any additional testimony
or confirmation? And especially when we think of the great
difference that exists between external visible action and internal spiritual relationship, does not the visible action detract
from the real meaning of the spiritual relation? It is here that
we must guard against our own reasoning and appreciate the
wisdom and goodness of God. God condescends to our weak-
ness. He not only unites His people to Christ but He also
advertises that great truth by an ordinance which portrays
visibly to our senses the reality of this grace. It is a testimony
which God has been pleased to give to us so that we may the
better understand the high privilege of union with the Father
and the Son and the Holy Spirit. This is the purpose of
baptism as a *sign*. And what is its purpose as *seal*? As seal
it authenticates, confirms, guarantees the reality and security
of this covenant grace. It is not indeed indispensable to the
grace sealed; the grace exists prior to the seal and the seal
does not produce the grace sealed. But just as God confirmed
His promise to Noah by the bow in the cloud and confirmed
His promise to Abraham by the interposition of an oath, so
He confirms to us the reality and security of the highest of
spiritual relationships by adding the seal of baptism. God
does not need baptism to confirm Himself in His faithfulness.
It is additional certification with which He provides *us* so
that we may thereby be confirmed in the faith of His grace.
He thereby shows more abundantly the immutability of the
covenant relation in order that we may have strong consola-

representatives of the evangelical tradition. *Cf., e. g.,* Charles Hodge:
Systematic Theology, III, pp. 591 ff.; Thomas McCrie: *Lectures on Christian
Baptism* (Edinburgh, 1850), pp. 13 ff., pp. 157 ff.; Thomas Blake: *The
Covenant Sealed* (London, 1655), Chapter XI; William Cunningham:
op. cit., pp. 241 ff.

tion. It is strange blindness that will not perceive and appreciate the wisdom and goodness of such an institution, and it is a strange underestimation of our need that will not discern its preceptive necessity.

It has appeared to many paedobaptists that it is necessary to distinguish between the efficacy of baptism as it applies to adults and as it applies to infants.[45] There does not seem to

[45] The present writer is aware of the difficulty and appreciates the attempts made to resolve the difficulty by some of the ablest of Reformed theologians. William Cunningham and James Bannerman, for example, maintained that a line of discrimination must be drawn, in reference to this matter, between the baptism of infants and the baptism of adults (cf. William Cunningham: op. cit., pp. 245 ff.; James Bannerman: op. cit., pp. 106 ff.). It may be quite correct to say with Cunningham that adult baptism is "that from which mainly and principally we should form our conceptions of what baptism is and means, and was intended to accomplish" (op. cit., p. 246) and that adult baptism affords "the proper fundamental type of the ordinance" (p. 247). The teaching of the New Testament in respect of the efficacy of baptism appears, in the main, in connection with address directed to adults in urging upon them the implications of baptism. But when Cunningham says that "it is adult baptism alone which embodies and brings out the full idea of the ordinance" (p. 246), or when Bannerman says that "it is an error . . . to make Baptism applicable in the same sense and to the same extent to infants and to adults" (p. 109), there does not appear to be good warrant for such discrimination. Furthermore, Bannerman's distinction between the right of property and the right of possession, by which he maintains that the baptism of infants has reference only to the right of property in the covenant as distinguished from the right of possession, does not seem to rest upon the requisite Biblical data. In the case of the infant he considers baptism to be "a prospective seal in connection with the faith which he has not at the moment, but which he may have afterwards" (p. 116). It is true that infants are not capable of faith and repentance in the sense in which such are predicated of adults. And it is quite true that infants cannot lay their hands upon the right which baptism signifies and plead it in faith (cf. pp. 115 f.). But this type of argument for distinguishing between the efficacy of infant baptism and adult baptism appears to rest upon a fallacy, namely, the fallacy of failing to lay sufficient emphasis upon the fact that that which is signified and sealed by baptism is not necessarily mediated by the intelligent exercise of faith and repentance. That which is signified by baptism, namely, union with Christ, regeneration, and justification, is not in the case of infants mediated by intelligent faith. Yet infants may possess these graces to the fullest extent. Infants may have full possession of that which baptism signifies, and it is the possession that baptism signifies and seals.

Again, we are not to take for granted that adult baptism, as distinguished

be good warrant for this distinction. Baptism has one import, and it bears this same import whether it is dispensed to adults or to infants. It signifies union with Christ, purifying from the pollution of sin by regeneration of the Spirit, and purifying from the guilt of sin by the blood of Christ. It can have no other import for infants than this. As a sign and seal of such grace the sign and seal must have the same efficacy for infants as for adults. It is, of course, true that in the case of adults the possession of the grace signified and sealed is inseparable from the exercise of intelligent faith and repentance. And in administering baptism to adults the church requires

from infant baptism, *necessarily* provides us with the fundamental type of baptism. Was this true in the case of circumcision? And we are not by any means to take for granted that the references to the import and efficacy of baptism in the New Testament appear only in connection with those who were baptised as adults.

If we think of the *prospective* reference in baptism, we must bear in mind that it has a prospective reference both to infants and adults. That which is sealed by baptism has many implications for the future. Baptism as the seal of union with Christ is the seal of God's covenant faithfulness and the pledge of our fidelity to the God of covenant. Hence it looks forward to the ever-increasing realisation of God's favour and blessing. In a word, it is prospective of the full fruition of the covenant relation which it seals. But *principially* infants and adults are in the same position regarding such a prospect.

The sum total of the evidence relevant to this question would not appear to support the contention that in the matter of efficacy we may distinguish between infant and adult baptism.

There is a statement in Calvin that might be appealed to in support of this distinction which we are now controverting. It is to the effect that infants "are baptised into future repentance and faith; for though these graces have not yet been formed in them, the seed of both lies hid in them by the secret operation of the Spirit" (*Inst.* IV, xvi, 20; *cf.* J. K. S. Reid in *Scottish Journal of Theology*, June, 1950, p. 172). It is not so clear, however, that Calvin would espouse this hard and fast line of distinction which we are now considering. For Calvin in this very connection lays great emphasis upon the fact that infants "now receive some portion of that grace, of which they will ere long enjoy the full abundance" (*Inst.* IV, xvi, 19), and that infants now may be irradiated with faint rays of what will in heaven illuminate them with full splendour. He makes allowance for the distinction between infants and adults in respect of experience and knowledge, but the direction of his thought is to distinguish between germ and full growth and not between efficacy in the respective cases.

an intelligent and credible confession of such faith. The possession of the grace signified by baptism does not presuppose in the case of infants the exercise of intelligent faith and repentance: they are not yet psychologically capable of such. And the church cannot require any intelligent and credible profession on their part. The accompaniments of the grace signified by baptism and the prerequisites for its administration differ in the respective cases. But it is a mistake to think that the import or signification differs. Baptism signifies union with Christ and membership in his body. It means this for both adults and infants. And so, in respect of efficacy, baptism is for infants precisely what it is for adults, namely, the divine testimony to their union with Christ and the divine certification and authentication of this great truth. Though infants are not capable of the intelligent exercise of faith, they are, nevertheless, susceptible to God's efficacious grace in uniting them to Christ, in regenerating them by His Spirit, and in sprinkling them with the blood of His Son. This grace, in the bonds of an everlasting covenant, infants may fully possess. This is what baptism signifies and seals, and no warrant can be elicited for the assumption that in respect of efficacy this sign or seal has any other effect in the case of infants than in the case of adults. The efficacy of baptism in all cases is that it is God's testimony to and seal upon the reality and security of the grace which He bestows in accordance with the provisions of the covenant of grace. And this grace is nothing less than union with the three persons of the Godhead in the unity expressed by their joint possession of the one name and in the richness of the distinctive relationship which each person of the Godhead sustains to the people of God in the economy of the covenant of grace.

It is germane to the question of the efficacy of baptism to ask: what comfort may we derive from baptism, both as respects our own baptism and the baptism of the infant seed of believers? What needs to be stressed in this connection is that we may never divorce the faith of God's covenant grace from the discharge of those obligations which inhere in the covenant relation. Covenant privilege always entails covenant responsibility. And this is just saying that the comfort and confidence of God's covenant mercy may never be severed from covenant keeping. It is an abuse that turns the grace of God into lasciviousness to divorce faith from piety and obedience. Faith severed from obedience is presumption, just as formal obedience severed from faith is self-righteousness. This principle needs to be applied to both aspects of the question, the comfort derived from our own baptism and the comfort we entertain with reference to infants.

To suppose that we may entertain any confidence respecting the covenant grace signified and sealed by our baptism, if we are destitute of godly fear, if we break God's covenant, and walk contrary to his commandments, would be contradiction. The fear of the Lord, the keeping of his covenant, and obedience to his commandments are the means through which and the conditions upon which those who have received the pledge of God's faithfulness may entertain the assurance and comfort of His faithfulness. To divorce faith and assurance of faith from fidelity to our covenant engagements is to be guilty of an abstraction which does not exist in God's arrangements. And faith exercised in such abstraction is not the faith of God's elect but the presumption that will at the end receive the rebuke of disillusionment, "I know you not whence ye are; depart from me, all ye workers of iniquity" (Luke 13:27).

Hence the sign and seal of baptism can be no pledge or guarantee to us of that which baptism signifies except as we are mindful of God's covenant, embrace its promises, discharge its obligations, and lay hold in faith upon the covenant faithfulness of God. To think or believe in any other direction is to lapse into the error to which the Scripture answer is: "What shall we say then? Shall we continue in sin, that grace may abound? God forbid. We who died to sin, how shall we any longer live therein? Or are ye ignorant that as many of us as were baptised into Christ Jesus were baptised into his death? Therefore we were buried with him through baptism into death, in order that as Christ was raised from the dead through the glory of the Father, even so we also should walk in newness of life" (Rom. 6:1-4).

Respecting infant baptism we must ask: what comfort or assurance may we entertain regarding infants who have been baptised? In this connection, also, the same principle has to be noted and stressed. The Scripture does not extend to parents who have received baptism for their children, nor to the church of God, an assurance or guarantee that the children concerned are without condition the partakers of the grace signified and sealed by baptism. The faith of God's covenant grace and promise cannot be entertained in respect of children and children's children in abstraction from covenant keeping and faithfulness. To divorce the faith of God's promise from the faithful and persevering discharge of covenant obligations is presumption and mockery. The faith of God's covenant grace to children is always in a context. It always has an environment. For there are no abstractions in God's economy of mercy. The environment is, in a word, faithfulness. The degree of faith and assurance that God's promise to them will be fulfilled is proportionate to the extent to which the fear of God, the keeping of His covenant, and the doing of His commandments rule in the heart and life. Such faithfulness to God's covenant is an embracive commitment; it includes all that is involved in the bringing up of children in the nurture and admonition of the Lord, a nurture which is not simply Christian but a nurture which is administered by the Lord Himself and of which parents are but the delegated instruments or intermediaries of execution. This nurture is the means through which God's covenant grace and promise come to realisation and fruition. And faith abstracted from the devoted and sustained discharge of such nurture is not the faith of God's covenant Word.

While the nature of baptism warns us against abuse and, when properly interpreted, precludes all presumptuous wresting of God's promise, yet the ordinance of infant baptism is intended to encourage and confirm faith in the covenant faithfulness of God. Baptism is the sign and pledge and seal that God's mercy is from everlasting to everlasting upon them that fear Him and His righteousness unto children's children. Infant baptism is one of the ways in which God assures us that the method of His saving and sanctifying operations in the world is not atomistic. The administration of His lovingkindness takes account of the solidarity in accordance with which He has created and governs the human race. The race is not a mere aggregate of the individuals comprised in it.

There are institutions in terms of which the members of the race sustain corporate relations to one another. The most basic of such institutions is the family and, as far as the history and government of this world are concerned, the solidarity established in the family is indestructible. Sin has, indeed, corrupted this relationship, and the solidarity is the medium through which sin is accentuated and aggravated. God visits the iniquities of the fathers upon the children unto the third and fourth generation of them that hate Him (*cf.* Exod. 20:5). The solidarity is thus not annulled. And the marvel of God's grace is that as redemption supervenes upon the wreck and ruin of sin it flows in the channel of that very same solidarity which exists by divine institution, an institution which sin has corrupted but has not destroyed. God deals savingly with men in their organic corporate relationships. He shows lovingkindness unto thousands of them that love Him and keep His commandments (*cf.* Exod. 20:6). "The mercy of the Lord is from everlasting to everlasting upon them that fear him, and his righteousness unto children's children; to such as keep his covenant, and to those that remember his precepts to do them" (Ps. 103:17, 18).

The more limited solidarity which exists in the family is embraced within a broader solidarity which God has established in the church. These two institutions, the family and the church, mutually minister to each other. In the operations of saving grace God fulfils His purposes in accordance with covenant provisions. One of these gracious provisions is that God is not only a God to the believer but also to his seed after him. It is in the faith of this institution, in the embrace of its promises, and in the discharge of its obligations that believing parents present their infant seed for baptism as the sign and seal of the covenant of grace. They commit them not only to God's care but also to His covenant faithfulness. The efficacy of infant baptism principally consists in this that it is to us the certification or seal that God works in accordance with this covenant provision and fulfils His covenant promises. It is, after all, the Lord's own nurture which infant baptism signifies and seals.